D1571087

PRIDE AND SOLIDARITY

PRIDE AND SOLIDARITY

A History of the Plumbers and Pipefitters

of Columbus, Ohio, 1889–1989

RICHARD SCHNEIROV

ILR Press

Ithaca, New York

Copyright © 1993 by Cornell University
All rights reserved
Text design by Kat Dalton
Library of Congress Cataloging-in-Publication Data
Schneirov, Richard.
Pride and solidarity : a history of the plumbers and pipefitters
of Columbus, Ohio, 1889–1989 / Richard Schneirov.
p. cm.
Includes bibliographical references and index.
ISBN 0-87546-306-1 (alk. paper) — ISBN 0-87546-307-X (pbk.)
1. United Association of Journeymen and Apprentices of the
Plumbing and Pipe Fitting Industry. Local 189 (Columbus, Ohio)—
History. 2. Trade-unions—Plumbers—Ohio—Columbus—History.
I. Title.
HD6515.P62U67   1993
331.88'196'0977157—dc20   92-47486

Copies may be ordered from bookstores or directly from

ILR Press
School of Industrial and Labor Relations
Cornell University
Ithaca, NY 14853-3901

Printed on acid-free paper in the United States of America

5   4   3   2   1

Contents

Preface

This book was conceived not by the author but by the members of the Columbus, Ohio, Local 189 of the United Association of Journeymen and Apprentices of the Plumbing and Pipe Fitting Industry of the United States and Canada (hereafter referred to as UA) in spring 1988. The plan was to create an instructional tool to impart knowledge and instill pride in the history of the local union among new journeymen, particularly students at the apprenticeship school. When the idea was endorsed at a meeting of the local, the union's financial secretary-treasurer, Charles Gronbach, was instructed to contact a historian to research and write a full-scale history of the union for publication.

Upon accepting that responsibility, I soon decided that it would have to be a collaborative effort with the members of Local 189. First, though as a labor historian I knew the broad contours of the labor movement and was familiar with the construction industry through having written a book on the Chicago carpenters' union, I knew very little about the plumbing and pipefitting trade and had to rely extensively on observation and conversation with those actually involved in the work. Second, there were almost no written or published sources on the history of the union beyond rather sketchy minutes. Thus huge gaps in the historical record existed that could be filled in only by interviews and informal conversations with veteran union members.

But the most important reason this book is a collaborative venture is that I intended it to be more than a coffee-table book filled with pictures and dry facts, a book that people point to but which no one reads. For those earnest and dedicated members who were troubled about the present but strongly committed to the future of the union, I wanted to write an accessible history that would help members draw on their past to think critically and creatively about their present predicament and future challenges. This, however, could be done only by gathering, systematizing, and making intelligible the memories of the past and the aspirations for the future of local members and officers.

During the year I researched and wrote this book I visited a variety of construction sites to observe work going on; went out in the field with business agents; attended many union meetings, a hall dedication, and the annual picnic and Halloween dance; and conducted and taped more than twenty extended interviews with local members, sometimes in their homes, sometimes over a beer after a union meeting, mostly at the union hall during working hours.

The narrative history in this book is the result of a dialogue between me—a sympathetic and pro-union academic and outsider—and the members of the local union. But I have also tried to let the members speak for themselves as much as possible. To avoid digressing excessively from the narrative I have prepared two non-narrative chapters. These are chapter 1, which consists of detailed descriptions to acquaint the reader with the work- and union-related lives of local members in a variety of settings, and chapter 6, which contains interviews in which six union members discuss their life stories as members of the craft and the union. The four middle chapters provide the narrative history of the local from its beginning in 1889 through its first one hundred years of existence.

Acknowledgments

Through an association lasting over a year, I have developed a great deal of respect, admiration, and affection for the members of Local 189 of the United Association. This book is largely a cooperative venture with the local's members and officers. The following individuals provided me with many hours of conversation and, in most cases, formal taped interviews about the history and the inner workings of the local: Bill Arrowood, John J. Bowser, Mike Bowser, Gene Brewer, Bob Dyer, Vic Eley, Pat Ferry, Tom Fetter, Colin Ford, Charlie Gaston, Mike Ginley, Jr., Charles Gronbach, Alan Hale, Jane Heinmiller, Paul Heinmiller, Tim Karrer, Mike Kelley, Ted Lancia, Dave Maxwell, Gene Minix, Bob Meredith, Greg Murphy, John "Gus" Naegele, Dick Patterson, Willie Santanich, Bob Schneider, Fred Scolieri, Bill Steinhauser, Louis Volpe, Jim Weaver, Francis Wolfe, Bill Worth, and Carl Zabonik. I also want to thank the following members for sharing an intimate glimpse into their lives: Teri Warren Dominguez, David Hinojosa, Albert Kirk, Fred Scolieri, John Waltz, and Francis Wolfe. In preparing the final version of the manuscript I have worked especially closely with business manager Gene Minix, financial secretary-treasurer Charlie Gronbach, Ohio state organizer Bob Dyer, apprenticeship coordinator Dick Patterson, and retired member Francis Wolfe. Allen Zak's photography was an outstanding addition to this book. I thank the local for donating the use of its photos documenting the local's history.

Among employers and their representatives I have greatly benefited from interviews with James Croson, Matt Roberts, Sam Shuman, and Ernie Ware. In particular, I thank the Limbach Company and superintendent Paul Gronbach and the Aries-Duckworth Company for allowing me to visit buildings in the course of construction.

The research for the book could not have been completed without the cooperation of the UA headquarters in Washington, D.C. In particular, I benefited from the unstinting assistance of archivist Mary Ann Coyle in locating records. Conversations with Coyle helped me clarify important interpretive points. I also learned from interviews with national training director Allyn Parmenter and assistant director George Bliss.

On the academic side I want to acknowledge my gratitude to Professor Warren R. Van Tine of the History Department of the Ohio State University, who convinced me to accept the challenge of writing this history and together with Charles Gronbach helped cement the financial arrangements for the project. Professor Van Tine read the final manuscript and offered valuable suggestions. Graduate students Toby Rosenthal, John P. Enyeart, and Philip Payne helped in a variety of research tasks. In turning this manuscript into a book, I have enjoyed working with ILR Press director Fran Benson and have benefited from the aid of Patty Peltekos, Trudie Calvert, and two reviewers who provided helpful comments about the manuscript.

To those individuals who contributed to this book and whose names I have inadvertently omitted, I apologize. Finally, I want to absolve the above named individuals and the UA for any factual errors that may appear in this book. I accept full responsibility for the contents of this book as well as its overall interpretation.

Pride and Solidarity

Introduction

The central theme of this book is that unionized plumbers and pipefitters have simultaneously held two identities. On one hand, they are journeyman mechanics working in a craft community who have values, economic interests, and ways of working, which to a considerable degree they share with their employers. On the other hand, they are union brothers and sisters, part of a labor movement based on a common class identity, which they share with workers both inside and outside the construction industry. Each of these identities rests on distinct principles: the mechanic or craft identity based on pride in skill and workmanship and the union identity based on equality and class solidarity, on that venerable ethical principle first popularized by the Knights of Labor in the nineteenth century: "An injury to one is the concern of all."

These two identities are balanced and intertwined in the experiences and roles, past and present, of all craft unionists and, in particular, of the members of Local 189 of the United Association, whose history this book tells. But there also is a constant tug and sometimes an outright conflict between the two identities. Throughout the history recounted in this book, these two identities have at times been reconciled and at other times been in tension and conflict.

The Craft Identity

To any reader of this book not already familiar with the way work and business are carried on in the construction industry, the craft identity needs explanation. For at least a century Americans have been taught that the relentless trend of modern industrial civilization has been toward the standardization of products, the extension of the division of labor, the increasing mechanization of handwork, and the concentration of business activities in massively capitalized, highly bureaucratized corporations. In recent years, as corporations have decentralized and downsized, lopped off layers of middle management, and abandoned or modified mass production methods to become more flexible, the inevitability of these trends has been called into question. Increasingly, employers and observers of business trends are recognizing that craft labor, small-scale, flexible business organization, and small-batch production runs are not anachronisms—islands of obsolescence in a sea of progress—but viable, and in some cases superior, forms of industrial organization.

For over a century the construction industry has accommodated slowly and only partially to the dominant trends in industrial society and has remained a fundamental prototype of the craft world. Its character is defined by the nature of its product and its market. Building components have become increasingly standardized and mass produced, but buildings themselves must be built one at a time. Each building project is of temporary duration and requires a one-time-only constellation of materials and equipment, skills from a variety of trades, and coordination, planning, and management of resources from contractors, architects, and engineers. For these reasons the construction industry, though increasingly dominated by larger firms, has remained a haven for small- to medium-scale firms. In 1980 60 percent of all construction workers were employed by companies with fewer than fifty employees. The construction industry is fragmented and decentralized, consisting of contractors and subcontractors temporarily cooperating under the supervision of a general contractor and an architect for a single project and then going their separate ways.

Standardization and the division of labor have had a limited impact on construction workers. Although for well over a hundred years work increasingly has been removed from the building site to the factories and the division of labor has reduced the skills required in many crafts, craft skill remains very much alive and plays a strategic role in the production process of building. A great variety and hierarchy of craft skills are involved in construction work, ranging from those of the electricians and pipefitting trades at one extreme to those of the laborers and helpers at the other. Most trades require considerable skill. Craft skill is the capacity to perform a variety of irregular and unpredictable yet related manual tasks efficiently and productively. Because craft skills are constantly evolving and because each combination of tasks on each project is unique, highly skilled building trades workers such as plumbers and pipefitters must assimilate a set of related general principles during a period of apprenticeship and then apply these principles to particular circumstances as journeymen. Building trades journeymen are continually challenged to learn new skills and to apply old knowledge in new ways.

Building tradesmen take a deep pride in their workmanship and in the buildings they produce, a pride that is rare in occupations in which specialized skills are performed repetitively and in routine settings. The highest praise a skilled building trades worker such as a plumber or a pipefitter can receive is to be called "a good mechanic." It is common for them to point with satisfaction to the buildings they helped build. Because of their pride in their work and their high pay, building trades workers are an elite with tremendous prestige within the blue-collar world. They stand in contrast to the typical twentieth-century industrial worker who performs a simple, easily taught task day after day within a factory or office setting.

There is another characteristic of the world of craft in the building trades that is crucial to this study. Typically, skilled construction work involves a high degree of collaboration between journeymen on one hand and contractors and their representatives on the other. There are three reasons for this need for cooperative effort. First, because the design of each building is new, the precise organization of work is different for each job. The employer, therefore, is dependent on the journeymen, particularly the one who serves as foreman, to help design the work and to troubleshoot problems as they arise. The foreman, in turn, relies on the initiative of other journeymen to deal with details as they arise. Consequently, though journeymen may be dependent on the employer to pay their wage, the work process is, to a considerable degree, under joint control.

A second reason for cooperation is that journeymen and contractors have common interests and experiences. Most contractors are former journeymen, and many smaller contractors can expect to be journeymen again in their careers; they may also want their children to serve a stint as union apprentices and journeymen. To journeymen the barriers to entry into contracting are moderate. They know that they can be self-employed if they can pool a small sum of capital and are willing to endure the long hours, uncertainties, and headaches associated with contracting. One study of a large local of plumbers found that half the men had thought of entering business on their own at one time or another, though most had not done so. Even those union members who have never considered contracting have often bid independently on small jobs and are familiar with the psychology of being an entrepreneur.

Finally, construction workers *must* cooperate with their employer. Journeymen have no real job security. They may work anywhere from two to three weeks to three months or longer on a project until it is completed and then be "on the bench" for several months before they find another job. Moreover, they may be let go at any time if an employer thinks they are not productive. Many journeymen become semipermanent employees of construction firms but these arrangements include no collective bargaining provisions that protect their job security. Journeymen realize, therefore, that their livelihoods are dependent directly and constantly on their skills as mechanics and their abilities to be productive. If the journeyman cannot help the contractor make a profit, he or she will be back in the hall.

The National Joint Steamfitter-Pipefitter Apprenticeship Committee's handbook stresses to apprentices that "in an immediate and real sense you and your employers are partners. When one falls down, the other is hurt too." It counsels apprentices to develop "enthusiasm" and "the ability to communicate and cooperate effectively on the job," to strive for "constant self-improvement" and "excellence," and to commit themselves to improving the productivity of their employers.

Thus employer, supervisor, foreman, and journeyman share a common background. All are part of a craft community, and each performs a role that may change from one day to the next. Instead of the top-down, hierarchical relationships characteristic of work administered through large bureaucracies and so productive of impersonality and adversarialism, construction work tends to breed an ethic of cooperation among individuals based on mutual respect for craft knowledge, skill, and ingenuity.

Union Solidarity

The building worker does not live solely in the world of his or her craft. Since the early nineteenth century journeymen have experienced class distinctions. Despite common bonds with employers, most journeymen recognize that the wage bargain in the labor market is inherently unequal. Contractors own the means of work and the workers own only the capacity to work and must sell this capacity in order to live. The situation is analogous to that of a person wandering in the desert, who will offer virtually anything to one who owns a glass of water. Furthermore, once the unequal bargain is concluded, the worker becomes subjected to the unrestrained authority of the boss for the full workday. The unregulated competitive market among contractors often compels them to try to impose unlivable wages, long hours, and unsafe and unhealthful conditions on their journeymen. It also leads to the tendency for contractors to subdivide skilled tasks and allow apprenticeship to decline, thereby debasing the very craft world out of which they came and on which they depend. Little wonder that nineteenth century workers termed their condition "wage slavery."

The main principle of unionism is simple but powerful. By putting the collective strength of all organized workers behind the single journeyman in dealings with the boss, unions make more equal the wage bargain in the labor market and lend some autonomy and dignity to life on the job. Though some people may believe that unions are no longer necessary, so long as the bargain in the labor market is inherently unequal, journeymen will need unions to avoid a form of slavery.

In the last quarter of the nineteenth century, journeyman building trades workers in America began to establish permanent local and national unions. Included among them were the journeyman and apprentice plumbers, gas fitters, and steamfitters, who banded together in 1889 to establish the United Association. During the same period the various building tradesmen and the business agents they elected to police the labor market became aware of the need for solidarity among the different building trades to maintain the closed shop and to win demands of common interest such as the eight-hour day. During the 1890s construction workers in all major cities formed building trades councils and established the principle of respecting each other's picket lines during disputes or strikes. Two great accomplishments resulted from this solidarity. First, unions became powerful enough to be able to share control over the labor market with employers' associations. Second, building trades workers' national unions quickly became the single largest voice within—indeed the backbone of—the American Federation of Labor (AFL) during its formative period from 1886 through 1904.

Strong unions and sympathy action among the various trades enabled construction workers to win the eight-hour day, lasting wage increases, the abolition of piecework and subcontracting, and a significant degree of control over their everyday work lives by the turn of the century. Yet this impressive record was not the outcome of the class consciousness that was common among factory workers. Rather, the unionism of building trades workers was powerfully shaped by the same characteristics of the craft community that gave journeymen some common interests with employers.

In the nineteenth century the low barriers to entering the contracting business led to intense competitive pressures that large, stable contractors were unable to regulate. To provide a measure of standardization and stability in the cutthroat marketplace, the construction contractors ultimately relied on unions. By commanding the loyalty of most journeymen and standardizing wages, hours, and other conditions of employment through collective bargaining, unions could prevent the large contractors from being underbid by small, fly-by-night contractors whose labor costs were lower. In addition, establishing a high standard wage enabled the industry to attract and maintain a work force with skill and pride in its work. Through their business agents and hiring halls, unions acted as labor contractors, supplying skilled labor on demand. This arrangement provided the contractors with flexibility by relieving them of the need to keep highly skilled workers on the job when there was no work to do. Finally, the union, along with a minority of contractors, initiated and maintained apprenticeship programs to train and upgrade the skills of journeymen.

In sum, not only have construction unions protected their own members, but they have also helped protect the contractors from the irrationalities of the market. This relationship helps explain why most contractors, in contrast to employers in other industries, have tended throughout history to accept collective bargaining as both inevitable and good. It also explains why construction workers' unions are not as sharply antagonistic to their employers as many industrial unions are. All this is not intended to imply that there are not tensions and even animosities between unions and contractors, nor does it explain the rise of the nonunion sector of the industry in the 1970s and 1980s, which will be discussed in detail in chapter 5. But it does help us understand why over time contractors and building trades unions have established a tradition of nonadversarial conflict within a climate of cooperation.

Two further characteristics of construction unions are important. Building trades journeymen are among the most loyal and tightly knit of unionists, in large part because of their effectiveness in achieving collective bargaining gains for their members. Another reason is related to the nature of the industry. Although some construction workers are permanently employed by a particular contractor, many others change employers with every project. Even most permanent employees know that they might be let go at some time. As a result, journeymen retain a strong loyalty to their union and tend to build up friendships and engage in leisure activities with other union members rather than limiting their associations to the workplace. Thus unions in the building trades serve a cultural function in addition to those of skill maintenance and collective bargaining.

But tightly knit unions based on craft pride also face a real peril. In an attempt to preserve the integrity of the craft, high wages, and enough work for all their members, building trades unions often adopt strategies to exclude people from membership and to recruit informally from racially and ethnically based family and kinship networks. As a result, blacks, recent immigrants, and women have for many years been excluded from union membership. Once collective bargaining took hold, the exclusionist tendency also took the form of refusing thoroughly to organize the union's jurisdiction. These exclusionist tendencies have proved to be self-defeating. Although in the short run exclusivity may protect jobs, wages, and working conditions, in the long run it enables the nonunion sector in the industry to grow up based on the excluded workers. Thus one of the greatest strengths of the building trades unions is also one of its greatest weaknesses. Pride can turn into cliquishness when craft distinctiveness is not balanced with the principle of solidarity.

Throughout the history of craft unionism the strategy of exclusion has been balanced by the union leaders' advocacy of a class strategy built on the ideal of inclusiveness and solidarity, which has led to a policy of accepting into the union all who are capable of being hired by contractors whatever their degree of skill or social background. Building on the identity of journeymen as workers, the class strategy spurs broader ties of unity with other building trades workers and militancy in conflicts with employers. The great drawback of a class strategy, if pursued to its logical conclusion, is that journeymen will think that they have nothing in common with employing contractors, that union rules can be set up that will ruin a contractor's business, and that the union should protect people who lack the skills and pride to be good mechanics.

The above description of competing strategies in building trades unionism applies with particular force to the journeymen of the UA. Plumbers and pipefitters are among the most skilled of tradesmen and therefore need to be particularly careful to balance a craft with a class outlook. In contrast to many building tradesmen who have accepted a degradation of their craft, journeymen in the pipe trades remain highly trained and skilled in a distinct craft. Since World War II, accelerated technological change has given rise to specialties that have subdivided the craft, but its substance—joining pipes, whatever the method—remains as it always has been. Almost all UA journeymen possess the skill of pipe joining and therefore recognize their membership in a craft community. But UA journeymen are also loyal to their union because it is a source of friendships and leisure activities, because it keeps them informed of trends in the trade and industry, because it allows them to upgrade their skills in an ever-changing industry, because it allows them to travel to any part of the United States and Canada to obtain work, and because they realize that, without a union, competition would drive down wages and working conditions to levels that would debase their standard of living. Every plumber and pipefitter therefore has to balance two identities. He or she has to strive to be both a good mechanic within a craft community and a good union brother or sister within a labor movement.

The tensions between the joint commitments to craft and class, though usually reconcilable in each individual, have tended to divide the plumbers' and pipefitters' local union into two informal groups. One group consists of those journeymen who work steadily for one employer over an extended period of time. Often called "key men" or "steady Eddies," they have tended to serve as foremen and often become so familiar with the business end of the trade that they are able to make the jump to contractor. Though these journeymen are usually loyal to the union, they often place a higher value on satisfying the employers than do other journeymen. Journeymen whose employment is less stable constitute a different group. They rely for their security more on the union and its hiring hall and less on any particular employer. They place a higher value on enforcement of union rules, worker solidarity, and the use of the walkout to attain common ends.

These distinctions should not be overemphasized. Most journeymen, when they enter the trade, work for a variety of employers over a period of at least several years and later are employed steadily by one contracting firm. Insecurity in early work life inspires strong loyalty to the union even among permanent employees. Some journeymen, however, because of personal temperament, lack of commitment to the trade, or an informal blacklist as a result of their union activities, spend their entire work lives without a sustained employment tie to one contractor. These men, together with the younger journeymen, tend to be the mainstays of the union's class orientation.

Throughout its history Local 189 has undergone several major shifts in its center of gravity. During its formative period in the late nineteenth century, the union tended toward militancy and solidarity with other building trades and with the labor movement as a whole. It is significant that the first union of plumbers, gas fitters, and steamfitters in Columbus emerged not as part of an organizing drive by the UA but from the eight-hour-day movement sponsored by the American Federation of Labor. In 1902 the union entered an intimate collective bargaining relationship with the contractors' association based on an "exclusive agreement" in which the union agreed not to work for contractors that were not members of the association. Dissatisfaction with this agreement led to a violent and bitter strike in 1904, which represented the high point of militancy in the early union and of class antagonism between the union and the contractors. Following that strike, the union entered into a long period of stable and cooperative collective bargaining with the contractors, interrupted by a few minor strikes. During that era, while membership grew slowly, the plumbers and pipefitters consolidated their union and generally stayed aloof from institutions of solidarity such as the Building Trades Council (BTC).

The career of Local 5180's first president, Louis Bauman, provides a good example of how militancy could give way to a craft orientation. In 1894 Bauman served as vice-president of the Columbus Trades and Labor Assembly when that body committed itself to a radical Labor-Populist program. By the turn of the century Bauman had become a contractor and a leading member of the Master Plumbers Association. Yet by 1919 he was a journeyman again and an active member of the union.

Throughout most of the first two-thirds of the twentieth century the union was dominated by conservatives who were content to allow the contractors to dominate the employment relationship informally. But during and after World War II, large numbers of young workers, influenced by the labor militancy of the 1940s and the high economic expectations of the 1950s and 1960s, entered the trade. Within the union they challenged the rule of the conservatives, which had been based on the power of the employers' key men. They felt that the union could win greater economic gains because Columbus was experiencing unprecedented industrial expansion and business prosperity along with a shortage of skilled labor on the job market. Under the leadership of Dudley "Curley" Steiner and his associates, the union entered a long strike in 1967 that won it huge wage increases. Later, in several stages, the local set up the modern hiring hall system, which enforced significantly greater fairness in hiring and shifted the balance of power in the employment relationship away from the contractors.

But by the early 1970s, high wages, the prevalence of jurisdictional disputes, and enforcement of inflexible work rules had sapped the competitiveness of the union sector of the industry. The nonunion sector made steady inroads into previously union work by relying on many competent mechanics who had been excluded from the union. The growing numbers and the militancy of open-shop contractors is now the single greatest threat facing Local 189 and other building trades unions. Since the mid-1970s the union has given much greater attention to meeting the concerns of the contractors' association in becoming more competitive through givebacks in contracts, wage restraint, and joint efforts to promote the union sector of the industry. At the same time, the union has engaged in militant actions and "bottom-up" organizing in an effort to maintain the economic gains it won in the 1950s and 1960s.

More than ever before, the union now strives to balance the journeyman's dual identity of mechanic and union brother or sister, and it also strives to reconcile and balance the complementary strategies of union solidarity and cooperation with union contractors. Whether these efforts will restore the position of the union in the industry only the future will tell.

1. Windows into the Union

It is impossible to tell the history of UA Local 189 without conveying the great sense of pride and satisfaction that journeymen feel about what they do for a living. As the job descriptions that follow make clear, UA journeymen experience considerable autonomy and initiative in their work, and they enjoy the constant challenge of applying their knowledge to new situations. Job satisfaction also comes from making a tangible contribution to society that is on public view for all to see and from the camaraderie of being part of a tightly knit craft group. The description of the union meeting shows how this sense of camaraderie carries over into the union as well.

Yet two other situations described in this chapter indicate a troubling feeling that the contributions the plumbers and pipefitters make to their employers and the community are not being properly appreciated. Health and safety issues and especially the rise of construction firms using nonunion labor threaten Local 189 members' sense of well-being, pride, and faith in the future.

The Pipefitter

In Delaware, Ohio, on a frigid December day, two journeyman pipefitters working for the Limbach Company, Carl Zabonik and Bob Schneider, are installing new underground steam lines at Ohio Wesleyan College. In the boiler room they have secured two long sections of fiberglass pipe horizontally on waist-high sawhorses. Deliberately, they measure the correct length, saw off the excess, bevel the edges, and glue on flanges (the outer rims of the pipe). This pipe is used for condensate leading from another building to the boiler room.

The pipe, consisting of an inner carrying pipe and a protective outer sleeve, is made of fiberglass. For a steam condensate system this is a new application of fiberglass. Two months ago a manufacturer's representative from Michigan spent a full day with Carl and Bob explaining how to work with this pipe. Perhaps fifty years ago the pipe would have been made of black steel. A hand-held threading machine would have been used to cut threads on the pipe, and the ends then would be screwed together. This was a long, painstaking process; cutting a thread in a two-and-a-half- to twelve-inch pipe took from thirty minutes to one hour. And if the thread was cut improperly, everything had to be done again. During World War II electric arc welding began to replace threading. It saved time and the joint lasted longer. By the 1950s many members of the local had learned to weld. The use of fiberglass pipe was a second major transition for fitters in less than half a century. Its advantages were mainly in cost and in its ability to resist corrosion. Fiberglass condensate pipe is not primarily a labor-saving technology, as was plastic pipe when it was introduced in the home-building industry in the 1960s.

Carl Zabonik is a trim man of medium height; his puckish face, which seems always ready to break into a grin at one of his frequent off-color wisecracks, is framed by a graying beard. Carl has been a journeyman for almost twenty-five years and has worked for the Limbach Company for seventeen of them. He is what old-timers call a "steady Eddie," meaning that he doesn't change employers every time he completes a job as do some journeymen. The last time he availed himself of the union's hiring hall was in 1972. On this job Carl is the foreman and Bob Schneider is working under him. Bob, a twenty-seven-year-old journeyman, who looks considerably younger, doesn't speak much. Like many plumbers and fitters, he is from a family with a long tradition in the trade. He has been a mechanic since he learned to love working on cars when in high school. He has finished five years as an apprentice and is in his fourth year as a journeyman.

Carl and Bob exhibit none of the underlying tension between foreman and workman that often pervades factories and offices. Instead, there is easy banter interwoven with the technical talk they need to get the job done. In part, this camaraderie is because this is a small job on which two men must work closely together for many weeks, but it is also because both are members of the union and few Local 189 members will hold a foreman's job continuously for any length of time. Today's foreman was a journeyman two weeks ago, and the journeyman

A Local 189 member welds on the job.

might be a foreman on the next job. With that knowledge in the back of their minds, most members are careful to avoid situations that might result in hard feelings or lasting antagonism.

This is not to say that there are no pressures on the job. As foreman, Carl receives computer sheets from the Limbach Company telling him how many man-hours it will take to complete the installation of a given number of feet of steam and condensate pipe underground from one building to the next. It is his responsibility to complete the job within that time.

Once they have finished fitting indoors, Carl and Bob hoist the seventy-five-pound, four-inch pipe—much lighter than the old black steel ones—onto their shoulders and carry it outdoors, where a long trench dug by men from the operating engineers awaits it. The temperature is about twenty degrees, and the snow swirls in eddies around the two solitary figures as they lower the pipe into its bed with two heavy straps called fiber chokers. Neither Carl nor Bob wears a hat or gloves; even after an hour outside, Carl stands with his jacket open. After many years, he is oblivious to the cold. He conditions himself to bear this weather so he can more easily stand the colder temperatures that will arrive in January and February. That this is largely an acquired ability becomes evident when Bryan Cooper, an apprentice in his early twenties, walks up to get his instructions. Bryan, who has been an apprentice for only four months, is wearing a cap, gloves, and three layers of clothing with a jacket buttoned up to his chin—and he is cold.

Where the trench makes a ninety-degree turn, Carl and Bob join the pipe to an elbow-shaped fitting. To do this they need only their hands, a cable pulley called a come-along, and a short piece of wire Carl calls a burper. Trapped air where the rubber fitting on the outer sleeve of the pipe comes into contact with the elbow might create a bubble, allowing leakage of steam. Inserting the wire above one of the rubber fittings as the two edges are joined allows this air bubble to escape, thus ensuring an airtight fit. As the bubble escapes, it makes a distinct burping sound, which elicits half-satisfied, half-smirking smiles from the two mechanics.

The Plumber

It is early May, and the new state Bureau of Workmen's Compensation building, a thirty-two-story skyscraper on the corner of High and Spring streets in downtown Columbus, is halfway completed. As construction superintendents in white shirts stride importantly to and fro amid a cacophany of drilling, hammering, and shouting, two union plumbers employed by Aries-Duckworth are at work in the basement installing the pump and filter system for a large ornamental fountain that will grace the ground-floor atrium. Paul Heinmiller, sixty-two years old and father of eleven, comes from a family steeped in the trade—his father and four of his brothers were plumbers and his mother's father was Louis Bauman, a founder of the union that preceded Local 189 in the 1890s. Paul is high on a platform using hammer, chisel, and drill to cut two sleeves (holes for a pipe) in cinder block to let through two six-inch galvanized suction lines for recirculated water to maintain a steady flow to the fountain.

Ted Lancia, father of two children, a former nonunion workman who joined the union in 1981, stands nearby fabricating copper pipe for later use. Though Paul is

Paul Heinmiller is a bastion of Local 189 tradition.

the older of the two and has been a journeyman since 1948, by mutual agreement he does the rough work because it allows him to rest his legs, which are prone to cramping after standing long periods.

While Paul drills and chisels a hole for a sleeve to accommodate the pipe, Ted works at a tri-stand preparing a copper "T" and a "union" for installation of the fountain's circulating system. First, he cleans the pipe with an emery cloth, then uses a torch to melt lead-free solder (about 95 percent tin, 4.5 percent copper, and 0.5 percent silver) onto the end of the pipe, carefully wiping it with a cloth to create a smooth finish. This is called tinning. When the pipe has been tinned and the fitting cleaned, flux is applied to both, then heat is applied and more solder is fed into the joint. The already existing solder will "come to life" when the heat hits it, making a watertight fit.

Their steady work pace is suddenly broken when the superintendent of

Ted Lancia on the job.

mechanical work on the job, Mike Littleton, an overseer for mechanical work for Turner Construction—which has subcontracted the plumbing work to Aries-Duckworth—comes up and tells them that much of their work the past two weeks has been in vain. Because the architect's drawings had not arrived in time, a mistaken estimate led to the pipe being installed where a wall should be. "You haven't been drinking this morning?" Paul kids the superintendent. The three men talk for almost half an hour, mulling over what has to be done to rectify the situation: where pipes have to be moved, which holes need to be patched, and where new holes and pipes have to be installed.

They are working with six-inch galvanized pipe—all pipe used by the state of Ohio is steel, whereas comparable pipe used in the private sector is made of plastic—weighing almost 19 pounds a foot; one 14.5 foot section they are working with weighs 275 pounds and must be lifted by a chainfall (a manual lifting device).

The pipe must be threaded by machine and joined with a forty-eight-inch pipe wrench, which stands about as tall as a mature man. It is heavy as well as skilled work, and at least ten days will be needed to rectify the error. "It doesn't bother me too much," says Paul when asked about doing it all over again, "it's just another challenge."

Work like this used to be coordinated by the architect and the engineer when a major structure was built. But more and more the union journeymen, foremen, and superintendents are asked to decide on the job where to cut holes or install pipe and other equipment and how to coordinate the various tasks so the material will be there when it is needed. On this job, with some exceptions, Paul and Ted have determined the elevation and the routing of the pipe after consulting with their foreman and the Turner representatives.

A more typical plumber's task is being carried out by Bill Worth, a veteran working alone upstairs on the eighth floor installing toilets in a women's bathroom. "My own honest opinion is that the material we are putting in is junk," states Bill as he surveys a toilet bowl. "Most of it comes from an overseas firm which put out of business a respectable American company, Zern." Bill has worked steadily for Duckworth and later Aries-Duckworth for over thirty years.

There is an old saying that "plumbers do not bite their fingernails" because of the human waste they often cannot avoid. But union plumbers generally do not work for the small firms that do repair work. Their time is spent installing new fixtures and pipe, which is relatively clean work.

After the floor Bill had been working on was finished, two men cut a hole in it and installed carriers—cast-iron fittings with openings on each side to accommodate two toilets back to back. The carriers are bolted to the floor with eight quick bolts. Four horizontal bolts extending from the carriers will hold the weight of the toilets. First, Bill uses a knipper from the tile-setting trade to knock off excess wall tile to get a tight fit for his toilet. Then he affixes Permatex sealant to the male thread (a male thread is screwed inside a female thread) to prevent leakage. Later, an air test will confirm that the seal is tight. Then, in a deceptively easy-looking move, Bill grasps the toilet bowl and fits it onto the bolts, making sure it is plumb with the wall and cushioning it with a wedge from the hard floor, which could easily shatter it. "I haven't broke one in a couple of years, but it does happen," he admits. Later the space between the toilet and the wall will be caulked.

In these and other tasks Bill uses a variety of plumbers' tools: a chrome

Plumber Bill Worth.

wrench (with smooth jaws), a level, a hacksaw, a torch, solder and paste, pipe dope, and tubing or pipe cutters. To these he adds a small variety of "helpers": a homemade copper socket wrench, a used rule that he doesn't mind getting sealant on, and even his home kitchen knife.

Bill is not just an installer; he knows the principles behind each of the fixtures he works on and the details of the plumbing code, and he doesn't mind talking about them. He can tell you, for example, how many inches a vent must be above the bowl and what size pipe is required for a given number of toilets.

Once the bowl is snugly in place, he cuts a one-inch copper pipe that projects from the wall above the bowl to the proper length, cleans the end and solders an adapter onto it, then screws the flush valve to the adapter, which has a screw that acts as a shutoff valve. Adjoining it, he screws on a rubber vacuum breaker to keep contaminated water from backing up into the fresh water supply going through the flush valve. Installation of a toilet seat covered by a plastic protective sheet caps the job. All that is left to be done is the testing.

Control Work

It is a hot midsummer day, and Vic Ely is working in the boiler room of Adria Laboratory, an animal research firm on Post Road in Plain City, where he is installing a 100 percent fresh air-handling system. Vic is the son and employee of Jim Ely, a former president of Local 189 and a former employee of Honeywell. Jim Ely has been in business for himself as the owner and operator of Automatic Temperature and Process Systems for over fifteen years. The firm employs twelve men, all journeymen supplied by the local union. Vic, who is thirty-two years old and has a wife and two children, is from a family of pipefitters. Not only his father but his mother's father, his brother, and his brother's wife were or are in the trade.

Temperature control work is the active occupation of approximately 50 of the 1,250-member local and another 50 have the requisite skills but don't work regularly at it. They are employed by Honeywell, Johnson Controls, Landis & Gyr Power, and smaller service companies like Ely's outfit. Control work probably requires the greatest knowledge and variety of skills of any of the subcrafts within the local. As Vic puts it, "In temperature control work you have to have as much knowledge of electricity as of mechanical systems and pneumatic control. We're not licensed electricians, but an electrician generally can't make this work unless we tell him how." Temperature control work involves the starting and stopping of chilled water pumps, hot water pumps, damper switches and fans, and heating and air conditioning equipment, either electronically or pneumatically. It also involves controlling their temperatures. Generally the control man is the last one on the job, making sure everything works before he leaves.

The purpose of the air-handling system being installed on this job is to keep fresh the recirculated air being fed into the room where animals used for experimentation are being held. Like most units, this one is largely custom-made. Every building is different. "In ten years," says Vic, "I don't think I've ever done the exact same control system twice." Adria Labs has sent a sequence of operations to Vic's company. In such cases, Vic's father designs a blueprint for a control panel to match the sequence, and Vic reads the blueprint and builds the panel in the shop (in this case Vic's brother has done the work) and then installs

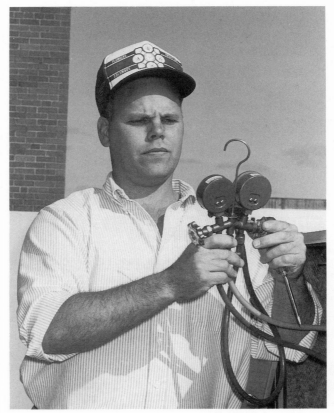

Vic Ely inspects a control mechanism.

it. The blueprint shows a heating and chill water valve, humidifier, fresh air dampers, face and bypass dampers, a freezestat, and a discharge controller. One page shows how the pneumatics are to be installed; on the other side is a diagram depicting the electrical portion of the same unit.

Vic takes about twenty minutes out to instruct a nonunion employee of Muetzel Plumbing how to install a chill water valve, a basic plumbing operation. With a pencil he draws a diagram on a piece of cardboard showing exactly what has to be done. Vic's questioner is an unapprenticed man who has been working at the trade for twenty years but lacks the self-confidence and sense of responsibility that come with apprenticeship and perhaps the experience of serving as a foreman.

Back at work, it is about ninety-five degrees in the boiler room when Vic makes the final tie-ins for a pneumatic control for the panel that had been "roughed in" (putting air lines in the general area where they will end up) by his brother earlier in the week. If the air-handling unit starts to overheat, a sensing device will either open up or close a damper through which air rushes past a steam coil. "People can say what they want about electronics," says Vic, "but pneumatics last a long time. It's not uncommon to go into school buildings forty to fifty years old and see the original pneumatic systems. You'll never see a computer today that'll last forty or fifty years. It's the most reliable source of control we've got."

Vic has a variety of tools, but his most valuable one is a tubing bender with which he can bend copper tubing any way he wants. It is a dying art but useful for pneumatics and still a staple in many United Association training schools. Half a century ago, copper tubing replaced galvanized tubing; now polyurethane plastic tubing competes with copper as the material of choice. But plastic must be run within conduit because it is vulnerable to being cut, and it does not look as nice as copper. It is important for the reputation of a journeyman and the firm he represents for his work to "look mechanical." "We get more comments," states Vic, "on the fact that our jobs look good than on anything else. When somebody opens up this panel, they're not immediately devastated by the way it looks. If it looks nice, they'll spend the time to look at it and see what it does. I've been on jobs where you open up panel doors and the plastic actually falls out of the panels. For a lot of people the theory is that as long as the door is closed, who's going to see it, who cares. Even though this panel may not work any differently than a bad-looking one, when you look at it, it looks like a mechanic did it."

Later Vic installs a freezestat, a low-temperature thermostat designed to detect a freezing condition so that if the unit gets too cold the fan will automatically shut off and keep cold air from being blown in. Then he installs a pneumatic sensor, which has a twenty-foot gas-charged capillary tube connected to it. The gas either expands or contracts, thus allowing the bellows to build up or bleed off the pneumatic signal. By the end of the day Vic has his air sensor, outside air and bypass damper, discharge sensor, and freezestat mounted and readied for final connection.

Refrigeration

The Limbach Company, which put in the HVAC (heating, ventilating, and air conditioning) at Wilder Elementary School in Westerville, has received a call from the school requesting that it repair two faulty exhaust fans on the roof. Tim

Karrer, a Local 189 member who has been in the trade for twenty-nine years, is heading out for the school on Route I-71 North in the van that Limbach provides for him and which he parks at home. Tim began learning the trade through correspondence while in high school; he was never apprenticed and he worked in the nonunion sector for twenty years before joining the union. Tim is trained in pipefitting as well as refrigeration repair and installation and can work at pipefitting when refrigeration service work is slow.

Refrigeration work, like control work, requires considerable knowledge of electricity as well as plumbing and pipefitting. About 75 percent of the challenges Tim faces on the job involve troubleshooting electrical matters. Refrigeration workers like Tim specialize in installing and maintaining refrigeration equipment. Compared to standard pipefitting work, refrigeration work involves longer hours, more stable, year-round employment, and the necessity of personal contact with customers.

When new equipment is installed, Tim works with the pipefitters who do the installation, the engineers, and others. He is the last man on the job because he must make sure all the connections are made and the equipment is working. "On every job it's always a little bit different," says Tim laconically. "It makes the job interesting. It's definitely not boring."

After conversing with the custodian of the school, Tim climbs a ladder to the roof, where he inspects the two fans. Tim shuts off the electricity—he is thankful that this is possible, having received shocks more than a few times—then removes the outer covering or shroud. The only tools Tim uses are a pair of channel locks, a couple of nut runners, a crescent wrench, and a screwdriver. He discovers that the fan wheel has been banged up, causing the fan to hit against the shroud, which causes the shaft to lock. The two exhaust fans cannot be adjusted and must be replaced. Tim scratches his head, wondering who beat on the fan wheel, which is new, causing it to freeze up. No matter; he calls Limbach to get the manufacturers' representative to order a new shaft and a new fan blade.

Back in the van, Tim returns to Columbus to investigate a possible problem with a huge refrigeration unit or "chiller" on top of a tall apartment building inhabited by senior citizens. When the chiller was put in, new, higher-output water pumps were installed but not new pipes. As a result, the scale that builds up in old pipes was knocked loose, causing the strainer to plug up. Tim was called in last week during an especially hot day when the air conditioning stopped working. Much to the relief of the tenants of the building, he made the repair and is now performing a check to see that everything is working. A quick check assures Tim that all is well. Half a day's work is almost completed, and it is time for lunch.

Health and Safety on the Job

During the afternoon of March 23, 1988, a twenty-seven-year-old female apprentice pipefitter named Tawnya Salyer was working for the Limbach Company on a large commercial building in downtown Columbus. Tawnya was the daughter of Joe Salyer, the owner of the contracting firm of Systems Mechanical and a dues-paying member of Local 189; her sister Theresa was a journeyman in the union. She was engaged to Tommy Schneider, a journeyman member of Local 189, and could look forward to a bright future. But on that day, for a reason that will never be known, she stepped backward from a large air handler without looking, tripped, and fell twenty feet. Tawnya died almost instantly from a fractured skull, the first female UA member in the United States to die in a construction accident. The local was in shock for many days. The Limbach Company was cited for three violations and fined $1,900. But the conditions under which Tawnya met her death were much the same as those faced by any pipefitter. Her death reminded every man and woman in the local of the mortal danger that lurks in wait for them each day on the job.

Before state and federal inspection of job safety conditions, members of the local walked off the job for the day when any construction worker fell. It was their way of calling attention to unsafe conditions. Following a different tradition that still holds, Local 189 members on the job took up a collection for Tawnya's family after her death, which resulted in establishment of a trust fund for her young son. Her family also received a $1,200 death benefit from the local.

According to the National Institute for Occupational Safety and Health, fully 20 percent of all job-related accidents occurring annually in the United States are in construction work. Since 1947, 47,500 construction workers have died on the job and 5 million have sustained serious injuries. Because inspection is lax, the situation is getting worse, not better. In 1969, when the Construction Safety Act was passed, construction workers made up 4 percent of the work force and accounted for 15 percent of the accidents. Today, construction workers constitute 5 percent of the work force and sustain 26 percent of the accidents. Each year 2,500 construction workers die; by contrast, 155 policemen were killed in the line of duty in the United States in 1988. Those who say that construction workers are overpaid probably do not realize the dangers they face.

Virtually everyone in the local has experienced some injury—usually minor—that is accepted philosophically as the price of the trade. Pipes and flanges fall on toes, dangerous gases and hazardous, sometimes toxic, substances are inhaled, sparks from a welding torch fly under one's shirt or mask—it's all part of the job. When on a construction site someone screams the word "headache," everyone covers up and backs up against the wall or under a catwalk. No one knows what item—a wrench or chain or piece of machinery—may come crashing down within the next second, but each person is too busy scrambling for safety to look up. For an anxious moment, each journeyman is alone; he or she can only hope and pray.

On September 8, 1987, William "Willie" J. Santanich was running aeration piping for a sludge tank that would agitate fecal waste at the Southerly Sewage Waste Water Treatment Plant being built for the city of Columbus. In a cramped area without handholds or guardrails, he had to walk on top of a ten-inch-wide concrete wall twenty-six feet above the concrete bottom of the empty pit. "Everyone knew it was unsafe," remembers Willie, "but construction workers know that sometimes if they won't work in an unsafe area, they won't work at all." Just two weeks earlier the contractor had fined a friend for refusing to work in an area that required a respirator because of possible contact with methane gas. Willie had a wife and two sons, aged fifteen and one, and had just taken out a mortgage on a new home.

He does not remember how it happened, but while he was walking on the ledge of that narrow wall, Willie slipped and fell. As he fell, he flipped himself in midair to avoid landing on his back and instead landed on his face. He suffered multiple and severe facial lacerations, contusions on his face and neck, a crushed left arm, four lost teeth, and massive internal bleeding. Only later did doctors discover a brain injury. When his wife came to the hospital, she was told that Willie was about to die. But he didn't; it was a "miracle," the doctors said. After being in critical condition for three weeks and undergoing five operations in six months, Willie is totally disabled, suffering from periodic loss of memory—what neurosurgeons call psychomotor deficit—and a permanent 35 percent loss of strength in his legs and arms. He now receives $376 a week from the state of Ohio under Workman's Compensation and $435 per month from Local 189's disability pension fund. But he will never work at construction again, nor can he

*Willie Santanich was totally disabled
in a construction accident.*

work at any job that would subject him to high stress. His wife now works; his savings are gone, and his house is in jeopardy. But he has not given up hope or stopped trying to recover a life with a future. Despite warnings from his doctors, Willie now attends Columbus State University studying accounting technology. "It wasn't a miracle that I lived," says Willie, reflecting on the fall, "but it will be a miracle if I survive."

In 1975 Mark Zack was a third-year apprentice, son of Arnold "Mike" Zack, an active, well-liked member of the union. On March 7 Mark was working for the H. K. Ferguson Company at the Anheuser–Busch Brewery. At 12:15 P.M. Mark noticed something strange. Two journeyman pipefitters from Local 189 had been welding in a holding tank. They were using argon gas, a shielding gas required for TIG welding (using continuous feed wire) stainless steel pipe. Argon is heavier than air and displaces it, and can literally cause a person to drown. Peering down into a holding tank, Mark and journeyman Roy Taylor saw two prone bodies. Taylor climbed down but was immediately overcome by the lack of oxygen and came back up. Then Mark climbed in and somehow lifted both men to the top of the tank, where they were pulled to safety. The two men recovered because of his prompt, selfless action, which merited a lifesaving award from the company.

A year later, Mark's apprenticeship class was having its year-end party at a lake. He heard the shouts of two apprentices whom he thought were drowning. Again without thought for his own safety, Mark jumped into the icy waters to save them. He was overcome by the cold and died of hypothermia.

Local 189 members take pride in the toughness that enables them to face danger every day on the job, and they take pride in the heroism of journeymen like Mark Zack. But there is a pervasive resentment, almost bitterness, among union members about the many injuries and health problems that stem from the carelessness, callousness, or greed of employers. It is reflected in the cynical saying that if you fall on the job, "you're replaced before you hit the ground" and in the oft-repeated complaint that journeymen are used like "dishrags and then thrown away." If the journeymen are "steady Eddies," employers usually demonstrate concern for their welfare. Otherwise, as business manager Gene Minix puts it: "They just call the hall and get another man. It's like a war; if you get killed, there's always another man behind you to carry on."

No single incident has crystallized this feeling more than the results of screenings done since 1987 for asbestosis and mesothylioma. Since early in this century construction workers have been handling asbestos products manufactured by the Johns Manville Corporation. The company's own records demonstrated that it was aware of the dangers of asbestos yet chose to ignore and cover up the findings. All the time pipefitters were handling asbestos without wearing masks and using asbestos for blanketing steam lines or protecting finished work from welding without taking any special precautions. They also had contact with asbestos insulation in the process of tearing up walls, ceilings, and floors. Workers in the 1960s and 1970s were the first to learn the fatal consequences of prolonged exposure to asbestos, and they brought thousands of claims against the company. In January 1989, six years after the company declared bankruptcy, a $3 billion trust fund was established for victims of diseases caused by exposure to asbestos.

The issue first came to the attention of Local 189 members in 1984, when doctors diagnosed George Hobart, a journeyman pipefitter, with plural mesothylioma, a fatal lung disease resulting in the progressive thickening of the lungs. Hobart died a painful, suffocating death. His appearance had deteriorated so much that just before his death he refused to allow any of his union buddies to come to his house to see him.

In February 1987, after several years of discussing the issue at union meetings, the local began arranging for x-ray screenings. A total of 467 members took tests, and of these 146 tested positive for asbestosis. Many have the plural thickening that can lead to mesothylioma. Most are now represented by a national group of lawyers specializing in asbestos lawsuits and can expect to receive some compensation from claims filed with the trust fund.

Those individuals testing positive can expect to get progressively worse over a period of years and may develop mesothylioma. This fear weighs heavily on the minds of many members, especially as more of their number die of mesothylioma. As Gene Minix puts it: "Once you get the mesothylioma you might just as well sign your death certificate because you're history. When you get that, these guys aren't living two or three months and it's real painful."

A Union Meeting

The regular union meeting is held every other Tuesday. The time is mid-January. The place is the union's headquarters at 1250 Kinnear Road, a spacious enclosure of which the meeting hall takes up only about one-third of the space. As is customary in winter, attendance is somewhat low, with about seventy-five men and two women present. Most are in neat, casual dress. They gather to chat in small groups until the president, Pat Ferry, gavels the meeting to order. On the platform, flanking the president on his right, sit the local's three business agents, Bill Steinhauser, Jim Young, and Bob Meredith. To the president's left, sit the recording secretary, Dave Maxwell, the financial secretary-treasurer, Charlie Gronbach, and the business manager, Gene Minix.

The president asks the sentries to be sure that no unauthorized persons are in attendance, then all stand to make the secret sign of the union. The president leads the group in the pledge of allegiance to the flag. In the final ritual of the opening, past president Fred Scolieri leads the assembly in a recital of the union's pledge:

> That I will not perform any act in any way prejudicial to the best interest of the
> United Association, but will at all times endeavor to promote its prosperity and

usefulness. . . . I will faithfully attend all meetings of the Local Union unless prevented by sickness or other causes beyond my control. I will at all times assist members of the United Association to the extent of my ability, defend them when unjustly treated or slandered, and cultivate for each and every member the warmest friendship and brotherly love. I will assist unfortunate or distressed members to procure employment.

President Ferry responds to the reading, admonishing the members in formal language to remember the pledge and treat each other as brothers.

After the previous meeting's minutes are read, committee reports are given. As was true eighty-nine years earlier, the first report is that of the sick committee. The chairman reads the name of each member who has been injured on the job or is in the hospital because of chronic illness. The list includes retired members, and each name brings nods of recognition and murmurs of concern. The committee can allocate up to $250 over six months to help tide over an incapacitated and needy member.

The most important portion of the meeting consists of the reports of the business agents, which inform the members of the state of business in the trade and the success of the union's contractors in controlling its share of that business. Each business agent is responsible for about one-third of the jurisdiction of the local. He must know which firms are bidding on which construction projects, who is hiring, how many jobs are available, and who is laying off and when. The reports are animated and elicit close attention from the members. Jim Young begins talking of developments in the eastern portion of Franklin County. He lists several upcoming construction projects that will begin in the spring. "We're losing jobs in the outlying areas," he cautions. The problem is that union contractors are not bidding, and he mentions a half-billion-dollar project in Gahanna on which no union contractors have bid. He asks rhetorically, Why are nonunion contractors taking jobs at such low bids? He encourages members to go into business for themselves to keep the work in the union family. "Some of our contractors are too fat," he complains.

Bill Steinhauser's report analyzes the problem of nonunion contractors winning a larger share of the bids. He explains that large builders avoid dealing with the union by farming out their construction work to developers, who then hire nonunion contractors. When the union complains, the builder, usually a large corporation that wants to avoid a head-on national battle with construction unions, replies that it had no part in the decision to go nonunion.

The union's paid officers: Bill Steinhauser, Gene Minix,
Charlie Gronbach, Bob Meredith, and Fred Scolieri.

The report of Bob Meredith, who is known among some members as "gloom and doom" Meredith, continues the parade of problems. "I've got good news and bad news," he says, introducing his report. "The good news is that there are hundreds of new jobs in my territory. The bad news is that they're all rat [nonunion]." He mentions a nonunion firm that "screwed up" a previous job putting in pipe for a local newspaper plant yet was awarded a fast-track (on a tight schedule) job on another large project. Jobs on a tight deadline are usually awarded to union contractors. The officers, Meredith announces, discussed setting up a picket line, but in the next breath he states that that probably would not work because the local building trades unions don't stick together. Nonunion work is like "a spreading cancer" in the trade. Somehow it must be cut out.

At this point one member, visibly frustrated and angry, is recognized by the president. Forcefully he takes up the officers' implicit challenge to the membership: "Things are coming to a head. There is a crisis in this local," he says, his face reddening. "Let's get the members off their butts or there won't be any more local." He is tired of hearing about the decline of union jobs. "Let's just get as many union guys as it takes and take care of business." Applause ripples through the hall. The atmosphere is suddenly tense. Meredith responds: "We'll never be strong enough to do this by ourselves, and if we set up a picket and other trades walk through it, our men get discouraged." The member shoots back that he is tired of hearing "the same crap. Let's get four hundred men and maybe we can wake up the union. We'll go to people's houses and drag the sons of bitches out. This is *your* local," he concludes, turning around. When he makes specific references to intimidation or violence against scabs, the enthusiasm in the hall diminishes perceptibly. Only scattered applause greets his last suggestion. The issue is dropped without further discussion. Members apparently think that as long as they are working there is no real crisis.

Next, financial secretary-treasurer Charlie Gronbach gives his report. Gronbach is often kidded good-naturedly about being tight with the local's money. He is called "El Cheapo." But the members like this trait in an officer who handles their dues money, and they trust him completely, reelecting him without opposition. But they don't appreciate the long, detailed financial reports he feels he must present to guard against the minority who fear their dues are being misspent. When he announces that this evening's report will be short, he is met by great applause and an anonymous "Thank God." After several minutes of decorous quiet, an undercurrent of restiveness begins to spread. Someone shouts, "Move we accept," even though the report is only half finished. Gronbach soon ends his litany of figures, and the officers' reports conclude with the low-key, half-mumbling Gene Minix, the real chief of the union in its day-to-day affairs. He spends most of his time recounting the testing that the union has initiated on behalf of members who may have contracted asbestosis as a result of long contact with asbestos.

Almost an hour and a half after the union meeting began, the "good and welfare" of the local comes up. Though most members listen respectfully to speakers who stand up to air their opinions, personal grievances, and suggestions, an undercurrent of restiveness that began during Charlie Gronbach's report continues. One younger member can be heard to remark that the beer is getting warm. When the president announces he will entertain a motion to adjourn, there is an unceremonious rush toward the rear of the hall, where beer on tap, pop, pretzels, potato chips, sausages, hot dogs, and cold cuts with bread and buns are laid out on a long table.

For most members this is the highlight of the evening. Renewing friendships over a beer and pretzels plays an important role in cementing relationships within the local. In contrast to many other union locals, those in the construction industry not only service their members' collective bargaining needs but act as cultural centers serving the leisure interests of their members. Local 189 holds several dances, a picnic, and a Michigan–Ohio State football game party each year and sponsors two baseball teams, a golf league, and a softball team. Probably at least half the members of the local are involved in at least one of these activities during the year. Thus considerably more than the 10 percent of the unionists who regularly attend twice-monthly meetings are active in the affairs of the union.

Confronting Sears

With a dozen members of Local 189 looking on, an angry executive from the Sears Roebuck and Company Northland Mall store addressed a squad of Columbus police officers asking them to arrest union members for handing out leaflets in front of his store. One officer listened respectfully and intently as the executive pointed his finger first at the police and then at the members of the local.

In early 1989 it was common knowledge that Sears was being pushed to the wall by nonunion discount houses like Walmart. That year Sears contemplated selling its tower in Chicago, cut retail prices, and instituted a series of cost-cutting measures. In Columbus, where it was building a large distribution center, it let the contract to Target Construction, a 100 percent nonunion firm. Soon after, it decided to cut costs on a new computer center by contracting its work out to the same firm, which then sub-bid the heating and air conditioning work out to another nonunion contractor, Tech Mech. Much of the rest of the work— about 60 percent, including the plumbing—remained union. In the past, Sears had used union labor for all its construction work, even maintenance. The contract arrangements for the computer center project, therefore, came as a shock to Columbus building trades unions, especially because Sears had assured the union contractors that there were no nonunion bidders for the project.

During a cold, slushy, miserable week in March, Local 189 members organized by business agent Bob Meredith began picketing the construction site. Sears refused to meet with the union so there was little else to do. The picket line was kept all day and was respected by all the other unionized construction workers. Teamsters coming in from Indianapolis turned their rigs around and went home; another trucker dropped his load at a storage warehouse. But then the general contractor instituted an oft-used union-busting tactic allowed under the Taft-Hartley Act. The "two-gate" system allows nonunion men to go through a separate gate from the union men. According to the law, the union can picket only the nonunion gate, which, of course, is futile because few nonunion men will respect a union picket line.

At this point, with Sears still refusing to talk, the local decided to leaflet three Sears stores. On April Fools' Day about fifty members, most of them between jobs, along with a dozen sheet metal workers, began passing out ten thousand handbills headed, "Don't Patronize Sears, Help Save the Jobs of Union Tradesmen." At Northland Mall twenty-five members, instructed not to respond to verbal abuse, assembled under Meredith's direction. Not five minutes had passed when Bill Lewis, a five-year member, was confronted by a well-groomed Sears store manager who told Lewis to give him all his handbills or he would go to jail. Lewis refused to surrender the bills and told the manager to call the police if he wanted to. The mall area outside the store is public property, and the union had been assured by its attorney, Vic Goodman, that handbilling was legal. But that meant nothing to the store manager. With the air of authority that is assumed by those accustomed to being obeyed without question, the manager told Meredith, "I *demand* that you get these people out of here *now,* or you're all going to jail. The Sears Company owns this property." When Meredith contradicted him, the manager spoke into a little walkie-talkie he carried, instructing his underlings to call the police, and then stalked off.

Meanwhile, many shoppers from this affluent northern part of Columbus were giving the union a surprisingly warm reception. Several older patrons went into the store and protested to Sears managers on the local's behalf. Many stopped and read the handbill all the way through. Others came up and spoke sympathetically about the union. A twenty-five-year-old man who said he had a secure job for life with a big corporation wanted to know how a union might affect him. The two union members with whom he spoke argued that "never is a long time." They reminded him of the takeovers of corporations and subsequent layoffs that were sweeping the country. They also talked of how unions help guarantee a high-wage economy, which is necessary to maintain economic prosperity. The young man scratched his head and thanked the men for talking to him and giving him something to think about.

About an hour into the handbilling three police cruisers arrived and officers conferred with the Sears manager, who was excitedly jabbing his finger in front of their faces. The police listened for about five minutes, then the officer pointed his finger in the manager's face, telling him the union was within its legal rights. The manager, his chin on his chest, walked back into the store. After informing Meredith that the protesters must not block entrances, the police left. Through all this time Sears security guards had been harassing the union handbillers. They told Local 189 members where they had to stand, brought out video cameras, and shot pictures from the roof of a building across the street. About 2 P.M., after more than four thousand handbills had been passed out, the group left, but not before informing Sears that they would be back every weekend until they were allowed to meet with someone who had authority over the construction project.

The following Monday the union's attorney filed an unfair labor practice against Sears for harassment. In return, Sears filed an unfair labor practice against the union. But the judge ruled for Local 189 because it had neither disturbed the peace nor littered. Within a week a Sears construction project manager from Chicago called, and almost two weeks after the handbilling Meredith and three other Columbus building trades union officials sat down with him to discuss the situation. Sears denied that it was taking an antiunion position, claiming that it let the project to a developer and did not know whether the labor employed would be union or nonunion. The union representatives pointed out quickly that the developer was a well-known antiunion firm.

Meredith meanwhile had done some research in Dun and Bradstreet and discovered that Tech Mech, which had a $5.5 million contract with Sears, had never before done work beyond the half-million-dollar range. The company also had a poor reputation for the work it had performed around Columbus. The Sears manager was taken aback by these revelations but said that a contract had been signed and there was nothing he could do.

In the ensuing weeks Tech Mech, relying on untrained nonunion fitters, fell further and further behind schedule. In June and July the union, assisted by state organizer Bob Dyer, decided to try to break Tech Mech by taking into the union its skilled welders and fitters, many of whom were doing supervisory work. Meredith and Dyer approached the men individually and told them they would be allowed to join the union if they would leave Tech Mech. Most jumped at the chance to join, or in some cases rejoin, the UA. Such an opportunity does not come often. More than a dozen men joined and were sent to work in nearby states. Taking the men into Local 189 normally would have aroused much opposition because it would have decreased the amount of work available to the typical member working out of the hall. By employing these new men outside the area, UA organizers avoided controversy. Toward the end of July, Tech Mech was finished; it closed up shop and returned to Indianapolis, and Sears reallocated the funds to union contractors to finish the job. Sears still has not committed itself to building with an all-union work force but has at least given assurances that it will allow union contractors to bid on future jobs.

2. The Power of Organization, 1889–1902

On November 15, 1889, approximately thirty-eight journeyman plumbers in Columbus, Ohio, organized a local union. The following August it received a charter from the American Federation of Labor as Federal Labor Union 5180. This much is clear from the records of the AFL. Four years earlier the journeymen had organized temporarily to oppose a pay cut, but the union established in 1889 was the first lasting organization of plumbers and pipefitters in Columbus. The following spring the gas and steamfitters decided to form their own union. In September 1890 sixty plumbers and fitters marched together in the Columbus Labor Day parade. The *Columbus Dispatch* reported that they "attracted attention from the fact that a very large percent of the members are young men, full of life, and were evidently proud of their organization." At the head of the contingent three men carried a large brass water faucet ornamented with a red, white, and blue ribbon.

Who were these men? What work did they do? What led them to establish their union? How successful was that union? These questions guide this chapter.

The Craft Skill of the Plumbers and Pipefitters

A clue to the meaning the union had for its members lay in the emblem of their craft borne so proudly during that early Labor Day parade. In part, the origin of this craft pride lay in a sense of antiquity, for the plumbing craft can be traced back to ancient Rome when early "workers in lead"—the literal meaning of the term *plumber*—fashioned the pipes for carrying water. But plumbers' pride stemmed not merely from a sense of continuity and stability but from a conviction that plumbing work contributed vitally to the well-being of the community. The union's purpose was not simply to push for higher wages and better conditions on the job, although those considerations were important. The plumbers, gas, and steamfitters prided themselves on their higher mission, which was to provide the public with high-quality light, heat, and sanitation.

In 1893 the United Association of Journeymen Plumbers, Gas Fitters, Steam Fitters, and Steam Fitters' Helpers of the United States and Canada (UA), founded in 1889, published its *Official Handbook*. The book identified the craft with advancing science, technology, urbanization, and service to a civilized community. As the *Handbook* put it: "The sanitary engineer, the plumbers, the medical expert investigating and improving sanitary conditions, hand in hand, will constantly minimize the dangers from improper sewerage conditions and the prevalence of various filth diseases, more particularly those of an epidemic character, will be greatly lessened."

In Columbus the union had scarcely gotten its feet on the ground when it began agitating for improved enforcement of the city's plumbing code. The code set minimal standards of sanitation, thereby securing the jobs of the members of the union, but the new organization could not have convinced the city government to pass such a code had self-interest been its only purpose. In this case self-interest clearly went hand in hand with public interest. The *Columbus Dispatch* paid tribute to the public contributions of the union when it referred to "the journeymen [plumbers] who have done so much to bring about proper sanitary conditions so far as their trade is concerned."

Another important truth about craft pride is vital to understanding the new union. Although plumbers and fitters could defend their traditional expertise, they were well aware that much of their work was the result of recent improvements in science and technology and that future improvements would create a demand for additional skills. This was particularly true of steamfitters, a trade that barely existed until the late nineteenth century, when America's industrial revolution was at its height. A description of the steamfitter's work noted:

> He is liable to be sent in to assist the construction of a refrigerating plant as a steam heating apparatus, a brine circulating cooling apparatus, or a hot water heating apparatus, or connecting a gas engine and a boiler. In fact, his work is liable to be part of a distributing system for steam, gas, hot water, cold water, air or any of the

various chemical compounds, gaseous, or liquid which may be moving with a velocity anywhere from that due to a pressure of less than an ounce per square foot, to that due to a pressure of from 5,000 to 6,000 pounds per square inch. In addition to the above, he is presumed to know more or less of electric matters, as the same is now used for power, light, regulation, and other purposes. In other words, he is supposed to be a sort of all around scientist, expert, engineer, mechanic, and common laborer, and all of these accomplishments are to be exercised for the benefit of the patron of his employer at journeyman's wages. In fact, the steam fitter of the present day is supposed to have as varied power and abilities as have been poetically ascribed to music, which hath charms to tame a savage, rend a rock, or split a cabbage.

The above account, written by a journeyman steamfitter, urged the young apprentice to "educate himself, not only in the practical everyday problems with which he has to deal, but with the underlying principles and theories involved in the mechanisms he is constructing" to keep abreast of technological advances.

In early America plumbers were all-purpose lead workers. They made a variety of articles out of lead and installed them in buildings. With the rise of cities and public sewage systems, plumbers became specialists in the conveyance of water and the removal of waste from homes and public buildings through the installation of pipes connecting to toilets. During the last third of the nineteenth century, plumbers ceased being employed in factories. They now plied their trade largely at the construction site. Still, the craft of working with lead remained viable because plumbers had to know the complex skill of "wiping joints"—that is, joining lead pipe with melted solder after shaping and fitting it.

The skill of the old-time plumber in working lead must be understood in detail to be appreciated by the outsider. In joining two lead pipes the plumber would straighten them by inserting an iron pipe and dropping the two several times, then lightly tapping a wood bobbin lubricated with stearine candle through the pipe. To prepare the pipe for tinning, which would make the solder adhere to the lead, he cleaned off oxidized material from both ends of the pipe using a shave hook. The plumber affixed gummed paper on either side of the shaved area to prevent the solder from tinning the unshaved area. Then he painted the gummed paper with plumber's soil, which he had hand-mixed meticulously from library paste, lamp black, and a shot or two of tobacco juice. Finally, the plumber heated a pot containing wiping solder. After the solder reached the desired tempera-ture—determined by use of a test paper—he poured the solder onto the joint with a ladle or splashed it on using a piece of wood lath. With the other hand he used a folded wiping cloth to shape the solder. To complete the operation the old-time plumber would often spit on the cloth to seal the bottom of the joint.

During the late nineteenth century the decline in the traditional skill of plumbers was counterbalanced by the need to learn new skills to be able to install complex systems of plumbing, particularly in industrial and commercial work. This, in turn, required at least a working knowledge of hydraulics, pneumatics, and the characteristics of a variety of metals. In 1896 the new handbook of the United Association devoted over one-half of its space to technical discussions of the changing craft. The concern of the Columbus plumbers and fitters for learning the latest methods was evident in the early 1890s, when one of the local's first acts was to establish a trade school for its members. The first subject taught was hot water circulation in kitchen stoves, ranges, and boilers, followed the next week by a discussion of venting (making an outlet for foul odors) from bathtubs.

Because the union did not seek mainly to hinder or halt technological innovation but instead identified itself with progress, one may well ask why unionism in the pipe trades came into existence during this period of rapid technological change. Finding the answer leads to a shift in focus, to the way changes in craft technology affected the trade itself, that is, the social and economic arrangements, including the labor market, through which work was carried on.

Though much of plumbing remained a skilled craft, an increasing proportion of the job could be done by unskilled laborers. When lead pipe was replaced by iron and later galvanized wrought pipe, new and easier methods of joining pipe were developed, most notably the threading of iron pipes instead of the wiping of lead joints. In addition, the advent of ready-made traps and other fixtures made installation an easier job. The incentive was now present for the plumbing or heating contractor to assign the less-skilled portions of the craft to lower-paid and less-skilled men. These men were drawn from the ranks of the traditional plumbers' and fitters' helpers and apprentices.

In the pre–Civil War days the apprentice plumber worked with the journeymen in the shop learning the complex and demanding tasks of fashioning materials—lead traps, for example—to be used on the construction site. To learn these skills, young boys willingly apprenticed themselves to journeymen for long periods. Helpers worked only on construction jobs and were not learners. They were often adults with few skills who assisted journeymen in the more arduous tasks of lifting pipes, carrying tools, and performing "rough work" such as knocking out walls. With the shift of shop work to large manufacturers and the consequent exile of the plumber with his apprentice to the construction site, the line between helper and apprentice increasingly blurred. Both became assistants in the work of the plumber and fitter, and both had similar opportunities to learn the intricacies of the craft.

As these changes became evident, boys entering the trade refused to bind themselves for four to five years to learn the craft at low wages. They reasoned that because journeyman plumbers normally required a helper on the job, they might become helpers at higher wages and learn the trade in a shorter time. By the 1880s the majority of boys and young men who wanted to learn the trade were helpers, not apprentices, even though the two terms were often used interchangeably. In the highly competitive economic environment of this period former helpers and apprentices with only limited experience were finding jobs in residential construction and in small shops that specialized in less-skilled tasks such as repair that paid at lower rates. The intercity railroad system that developed after the Civil War enabled these partially trained young men to travel to other cities and small towns and pass themselves off as journeymen. The result was an overcrowding of the trade with the consequent threat of degradation of craft standards and lowering of pay and working conditions. For example, in Chicago, the central city of the young UA, there were twelve hundred journeyman plumbers complemented by eighteen hundred lower-paid apprentices and helpers.

The ratio in Columbus was probably similar. The U.S. Census for 1890 listed 213 plumbers, gas, and steamfitters in the city. There were only about 100 journeymen in unions and almost all journeymen were unionized so that left an approximately equal number of apprentices and helpers. Another indication of the limited number of trained journeymen was that fully 55 percent of the city's plumbers and fitters were under the age of twenty-five and 69 percent were single.

Both the United Association and the local union in Columbus were formed in the same year, 1889, and for much the same purpose. Although the typical plumber and pipefitter in Columbus and elsewhere was not attempting to regulate technological innovations, he was concerned about how contractors had responded to technological change by hiring the oversupply of helpers, thus degrading the trade. As the preamble of the UA put it: "The objects of this association are to protect its members from unjust and injurious competition and secure unity of action among all workers at the trades." Thus both locally and nationally, the union sought to regulate the labor market. One means of regulation devised by the UA was to create a national system of working cards that would guarantee union journeymen employment and free movement across the United States and Canada, while hindering the movement of nonunion competitors who lacked skills. The second step, mentioned in the UA constitution, was to restore the distinction between apprentices and helpers and to limit the number of apprentices and the ease of their promotion to journeyman status. To implement this goal, the 1890 UA convention called for each state to create a formal apprenticeship system.

Organizing the Union in Columbus

In the 1880s Columbus was a swiftly growing government and commercial center. The population rose from 51,000 in 1880 to 125,000 in 1900. Coal oil lamps illuminated the city at night, and horse-drawn buggies plied the thoroughfares. On the street corners patent medicine sellers hawked "peruna," a locally manufactured serum, which a reformer called "the most conspicuous of all medical frauds." Perhaps the greatest reason for its popularity was that 25 percent of its volume consisted of alcohol.

Like the rest of America, Columbus was feeling the effects of the industrial revolution. Factories employing more than fifty persons were fast becoming the norm, and the smoke they emitted from the burning of coal cast a pall over the downtown. Among the new industries was shoe manufacturing, whose growth made Columbus one of the leading shoe manufacturing centers in the Midwest. The city's sewage system was only partially built, and in many streets garbage lay in open gutters. Besides manufacturing, a key to the city's growth was the streetcar, which at first was horse-drawn. By the early 1890s, after the city's first electric light company was chartered in 1887, the electric streetcar began to replace horses.

Not only did the city spread, but by the 1880s it was divided into neighborhoods segregated by class. The middle classes lived near Goodale, Schiller, and Franklin parks, while the rich fled the grime of the city to the areas around Capital University, Ohio State University, and Grandview. The two major working-class neighborhoods were ethnic enclaves south of downtown where industry was relocating. German Village, the center for breweries and small shops, was a tightly knit community with workers' singing and benevolent societies, churches and church-related schools, and ubiquitous saloons. Nearby was Flytown, more diverse in its ethnic makeup—the single largest group were the Irish—and poorer. It was home to the carriage-making industry, and the houses were densely packed. Columbus plumbers, gas, and steamfitters had ties to both these neighborhoods. Over 43 percent of all journeymen in the pipe trades had foreign-born parents, though only 9 percent had themselves been born abroad.

The city's early labor movement grew out of these neighborhoods, spurred by industrial development. Columbus had been an important center in the state for the labor movement since after the Civil War, when German workers founded the Arbeiter Verein (workers' association) and the city's trades unions had established the first assembly of local unions. In 1872 the National Labor Union chose Columbus as the site to launch the Labor Reform party. Five years later, following the first nationwide railroad strike in 1877, Columbus hosted the convention of the state's Workingmen's party. But it was only after 1881, when local affiliates of the Knights of Labor appeared and the Columbus Trades and Labor Assembly and a labor paper, *Union Advocate,* were founded, that the labor movement became a force in the city.

The city's wealthy and respectable classes did not accept the legitimacy of unions or collective bargaining. In December 1886, when the representatives of 150,000 workers from around the country gathered in Columbus to establish the American Federation of Labor, its first president, Samuel Gompers, got a taste of what Columbus city fathers thought about union organizing. When he tried to deliver a public address from the steps of the meeting hall, policemen prevented Gompers from speaking and led him away.

The eight-hour-day movement of the 1880s was a major watershed in the history of the American labor movement. The issue appealed to workers of all nationalities, races, trades, industries, skill levels, and genders. To workers facing threats to their job security from mechanization and cheap labor, a reduction of work time to eight hours promised to create 25 percent more jobs. To the typical worker, who labored from ten to fourteen hours a day, six days a week, the eight-hour day promised more time for family life, recreation, self-improvement, and participation in politics and government. For workers who sought to escape from wage slavery by forming their own cooperative businesses, the eight-hour day at ten hours' pay promised to shift the profits from idle capital to the producers, thus giving them the resources to go into business for themselves.

But for union activists the eight-hour issue was of absolutely crucial importance. Hitherto, they had only been able to mobilize large groups of workers for

Gas fitters, helpers, and apprentices, c. late 1890s.

short periods of time. The demand for the shorter workday proved to be the single most important issue that enabled them to mobilize and cement union sentiment and loyalty among large numbers of nonunion workers. It is no exaggeration to say that the eight-hour movement was almost synonymous with unionism in this era.

Because of its association with unionism, the eight-hour day was resisted fiercely by employers. On May 1, 1886, tens of thousands of workers participated in a national eight-hour strike. But three days later the hopes for a shorter workday were dimmed by a bombing in Haymarket Square in Chicago, which killed seven policemen. Seven anarchist leaders were arrested and four were hung in a fit of public hysteria, even though none had been involved in the bomb throwing. Employers quickly took advantage of the hysteria to deal the eight-hour movement a powerful setback. But by 1889–90 enthusiasm revived when the AFL called for a strike to establish the eight-hour day on May 1, 1890, and selected the carpenters' union to lead the charge.

The Columbus labor movement was slow to join this national movement, but in the winter of 1889–90 members of many of the building trades were expressing interest in forming unions where they did not exist and in creating a central organization to coordinate solidarity across trade lines. The movement was given a boost when Samuel Gompers returned to Columbus to speak on the eight-hour question.

The eight-hour issue sparked the formation of the first union of journeyman plumbers on November 15, 1889. Local 5180's first president was twenty-three-year-old Louis Bauman, a second-generation German, born in Columbus, residing in German Village. At the time of the formation of the union, Bauman had completed a four-year apprenticeship and was serving as a journeyman for Kelley and Company. He had been married for two years, and his wife was pregnant with their first child. The thirty-eight union plumbers, led by Bauman and officers Charles Zengler, George Kegelmeyer, and Edward P. Berk, held weekly meetings in a clubroom of the Wirtheim Building hoping to attract the two dozen or so journeymen who remained outside the fold. About twenty steam and gas fitters also began to meet in spring 1890 to consider whether to join the plumbers' union or to form a separate organization.

In August 1890, in the midst of deepening labor tension in Columbus caused by a strike of streetcar workers, the fledgling union demanded that their employers reduce their working hours from ten to nine. The master plumbers'

This Labor Day ribbon commemorated the first union in the pipe trades in Columbus.

association apparently wanted to avoid a conflict that they could not easily win in the current atmosphere. They conceded their journeymen's demand for a reduction in hours with no loss in pay. But in return, they asked the union to agree to a set of work rules. While a joint committee of representatives of bosses and journeymen discussed these rules, the union asked the advice of Samuel Gompers. In his letter of reply, Gompers rejected several of the rules, an indication of how inexperienced the Columbus plumbers were in matters of collective bargaining. He wrote:

> The proposition to have overtime commence at seven o'clock is entirely unfair and improper. In the first instance overtime should be entirely discouraged if it can possibly be avoided. To have overtime commence at seven o'clock merely means that you will work until seven o'clock whenever it suits that fancy of the employers;

and you will find that fancy to be, every day that you work. Overtime should commence immediately after your nine hours work; and if you have been in the habit of having time and a half for overtime and double time for Sunday it should continue in the same way.

After strenuous negotiating, the two sides reached an agreement, the first written and negotiated agreement in the history of the trade in Columbus. The creation of the city's first stable Building Trades Council helped motivate the employers' new willingness to bargain. Union leaders from the bricklayers, lathers, painters, carpenters, and tinners, as well as the plumbers and pipefitters, organized the council on the principle popularized by the Knights of Labor: "An injury to one is the concern of all." At the very moment when the master plumbers were giving in to the demand for nine hours, the BTC decided, in the words of the *Columbus Dispatch,* to opt for "radical measures" at the opening of the ensuing building season. The goal was to see that every branch of construction work was performed by union workmen. If this principle was not implemented, said the BTC, "the other trades will refuse to touch the job."

During the first two years of collective bargaining, there was good feeling between the boss plumbers and the union. The new union held its first and second annual balls and initiated new members. In March 1891 the *Columbus Dispatch* reported that the union embraced "all the first class plumbers in the city with scarcely an exception." Without success it attempted to secure the merger of the gas and steamfitters into the plumbers' union. It also explored the possibility of forming a national union of plumbers, but when the local leaders discovered the existence of the United Association, they decided to affiliate with it in April 1891. That year the plumbers became Local 57 of the UA, and in 1892 the gas and steamfitters joined as Local 61.

The eight-hour movement and affiliation with the American Federation of Labor had proven to be the impetus the plumbers and fitters had needed to establish their organization. But as the union became engaged in trade issues and affiliated with the UA, it changed its focus to emphasize the integrity of the craft. In 1892 the union moved forward on two fronts to ensure high standards in the trade. First, in February the union presented a bill through a friendly senator in the Ohio legislature to establish a plumbing code and a board of inspectors composed of practical plumbers so as to ensure compliance with the code. A union plumber spoke before the Columbus Trades and Labor Assembly to argue that "nearly all the houses that are built for renting purposes are fitted with bad plumbing causing disease and death." The *Columbus Dispatch* agreed, reporting that "there are some costly houses put up to be sold on the installment plan that would be ripped from cellar to garret if it was health instead of profit, that concerned the builder." The Trades and Labor Assembly responded by adopting unanimously a union resolution calling on the city to establish a plumbing code. Later, the assembly endorsed a local plumbers' union candidate for the post of city inspector.

The second front concerned the helper and apprentice question. The union accused two scab firms of employing helpers to do plumbers' work at wages below journeyman's scale. In spring 1892 the union asked the master plumbers to agree to an apprenticeship system governing the number and conduct of apprentices. The terms were not stated, but guidelines in the UA's strongest city, Chicago, suggested one apprentice per shop. The union also asked for a wage increase.

When the masters refused to answer a letter from the plumbers asking for a conference, the union inaugurated the first strike in the trade on August 29, 1892. Not only did the plumbers walk out, but the senior apprentices and helpers joined out of sympathy, and the gas and steamfitters vowed not to handle plumbers' tools. More than one hundred journeymen, apprentices, and helpers hit the streets. The bosses responded by withdrawing from collective bargaining and advertising for strikebreakers in five nearby cities. The atmosphere was tense in Columbus because the nation was already traumatized after reading of an armed confrontation at Andrew Carnegie's steel company at Homestead, Pennsylvania. The encounter between ten thousand workers and townspeople and a band of three hundred Pinkerton detectives brought up the Monongahela River by barge resulted in a bloody confrontation on July 6 that left more than a dozen men on each side dead and scores more wounded. At the time of the Columbus plumbers' strike, eight thousand state militia patrolled the streets of Homestead. Meanwhile, the steelworkers' cause had been taken up by the labor movement across the nation, including Columbus, where a representative of the Homestead workers spoke at the Labor Day parade.

To quiet the fears of the public, the plumbers' leaders pledged not to use violence against strikebreakers but rather to pay the expense of sending the scabs anywhere else in the United States. The strikers stationed a committee at the city's rail depot to watch arriving trains for scabs. All contractors outside the masters' association agreed to the union's terms, but the association contained the city's largest employers, and they refused to come to terms. The union had been encouraged by the BTC's adoption of the working card system to implement its closed-shop provisions more effectively. Unity within the BTC during the strike proved a vain hope, however, and several key unions withdrew from the council for trivial reasons. It was late in the building season so there was little work to be done and that could be accomplished by nonunion workmen supervised by a small number of scab journeymen and bosses. To make matters worse, the master plumbers were well disciplined in their own association and received support from the newly organized Master Builders Exchange of Columbus. On October 17 the Trades and Labor Assembly called a mass meeting of Columbus workers to support the plumbers but to no avail. A Local 57 leader angrily charged that the strike could have been disposed of "within a week" if the BTC had been working effectively. Finally, on November 28 the union called off the strike and the men returned to work without a contract, though most had won hefty wage increases.

The defeat did not diminish the loyalty of the men to their new union. As E. W. Mulford had put it in a letter in the November *UA Journal:* "The employers belonging to the Association say they will break up our Local Union, and make us knuckle down, but we say they shall not. There will be enough of us to stand shoulder to shoulder and hold our charter in spite of all the employers in the United States." By the fall of the next year the union had partially established by its own voluntary efforts what it had failed to establish by striking in 1892. In November, with Local 61's cooperation, it opened its own trade school with meetings every Friday evening. At the second meeting the city plumbing inspector instructed journeymen and apprentices on the guidelines for venting bathtubs. A year later the *Columbus Dispatch* reported that the trade school was "progressing nicely." The start of the severe depression of 1893–97, however, greatly strained the financial resources of the local. The trade school was not heard from after 1894.

Apparently to save expenses during the depression, the pipefitters' Local 61 submerged its identity into the plumbers' Local 57. It is likely that even at this early date the jurisdictional lines between the plumbers and fitters were not sharp and that many plumbers and fitters performed the same work, which may have facilitated the merger. The merger may have helped the union establish a hall of its own in 1894, which was furnished with a well-stocked library. In that same year the joint local attempted to set up a state association of plumbers and pipefitters. The *Columbus Dispatch* commented that the Columbus local was "one of the strongest unions in the state."

During this period the plumbers and pipefitters were active both in the BTC and in the Trades and Labor Assembly in attempting to secure broader solidarity with other workers during trade disputes and in advancing labor's political strength. In 1893 Louis Bauman served as vice-president of the Trades and Labor Assembly, and in 1894 he was president both of the plumbers' and pipefitters' Local 57 and of the assembly. Politically, Bauman was a Labor-Populist, aligned with radical farmers in the Farmers' Alliances and the national People's party and with the union men who felt that something should be done to change an economic system in which workingmen were impoverished while Wall Street banks and national corporations dominated the government.

In a speech to the assembly Bauman argued humorously that the tramp was "the only free man left in the country." What he meant was explained in the Declaration of Principles of the Columbus Trades and Labor Assembly's constitution adopted in 1894, the year he was president:

> It is self-evident that, as the power of capital combines and increases, the political freedom of the masses becomes more and more a delusive force. There can be no harmony between capital and labor under the present industrial system for the simple reason that capital, in its modern character, consists very largely of rent, interest, and profits, extorted from the producers, who possess neither the land nor the means of production, and are therefore compelled to sell their labor and brains or both to the possessor of the land and means of production at such prices as an uncertain and speculative market may allow. Organization of Trades and Labor Unions is one of the most effective means to check the evil outgrowths of the prevailing system.

The constitution went on to advocate the use of the ballot:

> Our only hope of industrial emancipation lies in alliance with the progressive political forces of the times. Our greatest error in the past has been in the support of parties pledged to the perpetuation of an industrial system which has produced an arrogant plutocracy and impoverished the common people.

During this period of depression and social and political upheaval, Columbus labor welcomed and gave support to Jacob Coxey, a Massilon quarry operator, and his "army" of unemployed workmen. Coxey's army billed itself as a marching "commonweal of Christ" that would deliver "a living petition" to Congress demanding a public works program to provide jobs. In 1894 the Columbus labor movement entered local politics, presenting a labor ticket that was badly defeated. On the national level the populist reform movement culminated with the Democratic party's nomination of William Jennings Bryan for president on a platform of free coinage of silver, vigorously endorsed by the Trades and Labor Assembly.

During the 1890s the strength of the labor movement rested heavily on the building trades unions. In contrast to unions in other industries, unions in construction were weakened but not destroyed by depression and unemployment. In 1898 the *Columbus Dispatch* reported that "the unions [of the BTC] have not been materially reduced in membership in the past three or four years of general business depression." Yet disunity continued to hamper Columbus's labor movement. Several times during this period the BTC and the Trades and Labor Assembly engaged in unseemly disputes that resulted in separate Labor Day parades. The plumbers and pipefitters withdrew from the assembly.

The return to prosperity in 1898 marked the end of a radical period in the Columbus labor movement's history. It was also the end of an era for the plumbers and pipefitters. For reasons that are unclear, in December 1898 Local 57 ceased to be listed in the Columbus business directory and in the UA's official journal as a functioning local. A union that survived the depression years was unlikely to have fallen prey to unemployment. More likely, the prolonged lack of a contract and the failure of apathetic members to pay dues caused the demise of the local.

The Birth of Locals 189 and 216

Columbus plumbers and pipefitters were not long without a functioning organization. Less than a year after the disintegration of Local 57, a small group of journeyman plumbers led by Michael Ginley, Martin Stai, Louis Bauman, Edward Mills, Thomas Martin, and Frank Tully met on July 17, 1899, in the back room of the Express Company to resuscitate the union. One week later, the committee on organization established a constitution setting out the purpose of the union—"for the betterment of the entire craft both socially and financially"—and stating that all members were required to pay dues of ten cents weekly and attend meetings regularly. By the following week twenty-eight members had signed the rolls of the new union.

Though the new union included prominent officers of old Local 57—Bauman, Charles Zengler, and Edward Berk—the organization was the product of new leadership. Mike Ginley, one of the founders, was from Marietta, Ohio. During the previous two years he had been in Florida helping construct military fortifications for the Spanish-American War. Like many others at the time, Ginley had learned plumbing as a helper; he was not from a family of plumbers and fitters. Ginley was a second-generation Irish Catholic who stood about five feet nine inches tall and weighed about 155 pounds; he was clean shaven, and wore glasses. He was a serious man, who regularly attended church and refused to indulge in drink. Though soft-spoken, he had a short temper and was known to be intolerant of drunk members "poppin' off on the floor of a meeting." During one early meeting he reputedly threw a drunk down the stairs of the union hall rather than suffer his interruptions. Ginley, like many early leaders, was a good speaker, and others listened to him with respect.

On July 31 the new union elected Martin Stai as its first president, Frank Tully as vice-president, Ginley as recording secretary; Edward Mills as financial secretary, and Louis Bauman as treasurer. According to the minutes, which still survive, twenty-three other members signed the rolls: Albert Lowe, John Rhorenbeck, Joseph Murphy, Peter Constable, Andrew J. Koehl, Thomas Birch, Thomas Martin, Charles Zengler, Harry Wheeler, Elmer Guilds, Harry Gibson, J. F. Brown, John Harris, James J. Dolan, Harry Williams, Edward P. Berk, Philip McGinnis, William F. Blair, J. W. Leonhardt, Edwin Wolf, William H. Seddon, Walter M. Turner, and Hugh Hamon.

During the next three months the new local set as its goal a minimum wage of $2.50 per day for journeymen and initiated one or two new members per week at a $1 initiation fee. After the local set up a committee to consider affiliating with the UA, on November 20, 1901, Mike Ginley collected $19 in initiation fees to join the national union. According to his own account, which has been passed on as lore within the union, Ginley made up the difference when he found that someone had put in a Mexican dollar. On December 9, 1899, the Columbus plumbers and steamfitters received a charter from the UA as Local 189. Soon afterward, with the local's consent, the UA granted the gas and steamfitters of Columbus a charter as Local 216.

Local 189 picked up where Local 57 had left off in the early 1890s, trying to

Michael Ginley, Sr., a founding father of Local 189.

establish control over the labor market through government enactment and stable collective bargaining relations with the contractors. During the winter of 1899–1900 the union lobbied with the state legislature against a plumbing code bill initiated by the Master Plumbers' Association (MPA). The union wanted equal representation with the masters on the examining board, a low license fee, and a practical plumber chosen as inspector. Though the Master Plumbers' Association made concessions to the union, Local 189 refused to compromise and withdrew its support for the bill, whereupon it died.

The cooperative attitude of the masters boded well for an agreement on other issues. In April a Local 189 committee began negotiations with a committee from the masters for a collective bargaining agreement that would gain for the union two key demands that had been issues in the 1890s. One was a reduction in hours from nine to eight with an increase in pay from the existing $2.50 to $3.00 per day. The other was the regulation of helpers and apprentices. The union also asked that the masters agree to hire only union plumbers. Local 189 presented five other propositions to the Master Plumbers' Association, among them a half-day holiday on Saturdays; overtime pay at time and a half except on Saturday nights, Sundays, and legal holidays, which were to be paid at double time; and pay for transportation and board for any member working outside the city.

In contrast to the early 1890s, the union now offered a lucrative incentive to the masters. In its letter to the contractors, Local 189 stated, "The journeymen plumbers of 189 wish to have an understanding with your association to hire none but Union Plumbers and we will in return work for none but members of your association." Such was the outline of the "exclusive agreement," which was pioneered in the plumbing trades in New York, Chicago, and other large cities in the 1890s. The exclusive agreement allowed the employers' association to regulate the fierce competition characteristic of the industry. By allowing the union to set standard rates for the trade, employers freed themselves of competition from smaller firms that might underbid them with cheap labor. The union's agreement to work only for association contractors created an important barrier to entry into the industry. All this depended, of course, on the success of the union in organizing the vast majority of skilled journeymen.

Many exclusive agreements contained clauses specifying that union members could not handle any materials not purchased by their immediate employers. In return, employers normally offered local unions benefits that they had great difficulty winning otherwise: a closed shop, the eight-hour day, and stable or increased wages.

In 1891 the UA had endorsed a model form of agreement, which was essentially an exclusive agreement. But by the late 1890s union leaders realized that this approach to collective bargaining had important drawbacks. First, it limited the employment opportunities of UA members. Contractors who paid union rates and observed union rules were to be denied union craftsmen simply because they were not allowed to become members of the employers' associations. Brewers and other manufacturing employers were compelled to deprive union men of jobs because the owners bought their own supplies. Second, the practice unduly strengthened employers' associations while undermining the freedom of action of the unions. In Chicago in 1899, after the contractors promulgated a series of principles that would undermine the unions' power at the workplace and compel them to abandon sympathy strikes, the plumbers and other unions in the Building Trades Council abrogated all exclusive agreements. This action precipitated a thirteen-month lockout in which the unions were defeated by the contractors and forced to dissolve the BTC.

As a result of these problems and the Chicago abrogation, UA president John S. Kelley publicly repudiated the idea of the exclusive agreement, though continued support for such agreements from many locals led the 1900 UA convention to refuse to legislate a total ban. This hesitant policy allowed exclusive agreements to continue into the early twentieth century in places like Columbus, where construction unionism and intertrade solidarity through the Building Trades Council were relatively weak.

Throughout the summer, fall, and winter of 1900–1901 a joint committee of Locals 189 and 216 met sporadically with the contractors. While negotiations dragged on, the union began to feel the need to reach out to its natural allies to prepare for a possible strike. The first step came in response to the formation of a state association of master plumbers and a dispute over nonunion work on a state of Ohio building project. The union decided it was time to cooperate with the Cleveland local to form a state association of plumbers and pipefitters. On April 1, 1901, five Ohio locals took part in a state convention held in Columbus to establish the Ohio State Association of Journeyman Plumbers, Pipefitters, Steam Fitters and Steam Fitters' Helpers. William Fischer of Local 216 served as the first association president. William Mangan of Local 189 served as the fourth vice-president. So weak were the unions that the new state association withheld the names of delegates from the press for fear that the contractors might blacklist them.

At the same time, Locals 189 and 216 revived their solidarity with the other building trades. During the spring of 1901 the carpenters were in the midst of a major strike that would determine their survival. By early May the carpenters were on the verge of requesting other trades to strike in solidarity wherever nonunion carpenters were employed. The situation threatened to become a general walkout because trades such as the plumbers and pipefitters had their own demands. The widespread sympathy for the carpenters among building trades workers led the plumbers and pipefitters and other trades to create a new Building Trades Council.

On March 25, Locals 189 and 216 applied to the UA for permission to strike; in the meantime, they launched a major organizing campaign to take in all men working at the trade, thus buttressing their ability to request an exclusive agreement. They lowered the initiation fee to $1 and asked each member to consider himself a committee of one to bring in nonunion men. Almost immediately, Local 189 accepted fifteen new members and elected them to membership in a mass ballot. During the Ohio State Association's convention in Columbus, the union delegates held an open meeting to attract local nonunion workmen and gained eighteen new members.

By early May there were close to eighty members in Local 189 and forty in Local 216. Faced with the new strength and unity of the plumbers and pipefitters and the prospect of united action by building tradesmen, the Master Plumbers' Association conceded most of the demands of the unions on May 6 in a two-year contract. According to William Carlisle of Local 216, writing in the *UA Journal*: "They really gave us more than we asked for. They gave eight hours for a day's work and they are not to employ plumbers or fitters that are not members of the UA. They are to employ only one senior apprentice to two journeymen and the journeymen are to get the preference. Where the wages had been ranging from $1.50 per day to $3, they gave us a minimum of $2.50. The wages paid to steam and gas fitters were from $1 to $2.75, so they agreed to a minimum wage of $2.25."

To help police this agreement, the two locals elected a joint business agent, Charles A. McAndrews, the first to serve in such a position in the trade in Columbus. His wage equaled that of a journeyman. Each member helped to compile a central list of apprentices in each shop, which was then used to implement the apprenticeship limit. In addition, the union compiled its first list of working rules that were to be supplementary to the agreement. On June 3, 1901, the union fulfilled its end of the bargain when it voted "to pull all members out of shops that are not members of the Master Plumbers' Association and that are not employing members in good standing." In return, contractors were expected to refuse to employ journeymen who did not pay dues to the local. In a supplement to the local contract, the Master Plumbers' Association agreed with the leading material suppliers, affiliated with the Central Supply Association, to use only materials it supplied.

In the first twelve years of the existence of unionism in the Columbus pipe trades two major tendencies—craft community and union solidarity—asserted themselves. Mobilized by the excitement of the eight-hour movement, plumbers and pipefitters had formed their first unions in 1889–90. Extending the principle of solidarity, they had joined with other building tradesmen to form the Building Trades Council. The viability of the Building Trades Council was a critical factor in determining the outcome of several strikes by plumbers and fitters in this period. Along with the union principle, the local sought to maintain the craft community. After the contractors refused to form an apprenticeship program, the union formed its own trade school and took the initiative in lobbying for a plumbing code. Local 189 was formed not only to better the lot of journeymen but, in the words of the constitution committee, for "the betterment of the entire craft." Thus Locals 189 and 216 successfully brought together the two principles that gave sustenance to craft unionism.

As late as February 1900 both locals had been on a precarious footing in the trade. In that month the union informed the owner of the union hall that "as far as we know we will stay here a year. That is, if we are in existence." A year and a half later the situation had improved dramatically. Both locals participated in the city's Labor Day parade, the members wearing expensive uniforms consisting of black shirt, blue overalls, black cap, and white necktie. Any member not turning out with the required uniform was subject to a stiff fine. It was an indication of the unity, sense of permanency, and craft and organizational pride that both locals possessed once they had a collective bargaining agreement.

Yet storm clouds hovered on the horizon. The exclusive agreement had taken the idea of the craft community too far, breaching basic principles of unionism. This imbalance would have to be remedied.

3. The Union Takes Shape, 1901–1945

During the turbulent 1880s, 1890s, and early years of the twentieth century, the plumbers and pipefitters of Columbus were involved in sometimes bitter conflict with their employers. Like other working people in Columbus they were part of an insurgent labor movement struggling for survival in a hostile environment. The fragility of the early union was evident in its initial reliance on the exclusive agreement, which strengthened the employers' association. Though Locals 189 and 216 soon abandoned the exclusive agreement, they also abandoned much of their willingness to fight for contract improvements and their solidarity with the rest of the labor movement. Both locals settled into a long-standing collective bargaining relationship with their employers, the main virtue of which was its stability.

Organizational Developments in Local 189

Throughout most of the nineteenth century unions were temporary organizations. They lacked collective bargaining agreements, stable leadership, and sustained loyalty from the rank and file. In most trades, even those with strong craft traditions like the pipe trades, unions often went out of existence following a lost strike, when work was scarce during a depression, or because of internal dissension. These factors had worked against Columbus Local 57 during the late 1890s. Labor activists—the "founding fathers" of the early unions—had to search for ways to stabilize and institutionalize their organizations. There were three major ways this goal could be accomplished, all of which are relevant to the development of Local 189. First, unions provided benefits in the form of a monetary incentive to members of the craft to stay with the union during good times and bad. Second, unions centralized many functions in the hands of a full-time, paid, professional leadership both on the local and national levels. Third, union leaders tried to foster a spirit of brotherhood to join the members in a tight fraternity.

In the late 1880s and 1890s many American craft unions discovered the secret that British unions had known since the 1850s: that low initiation fees, low dues, and few or no benefits created a union that was easy to join but also easy to quit. In contrast to factory hands, however, many craft workers received wages that allowed them to pay high dues and initiation fees and enjoy the advantages of a benefit system. Craft workers could see unionism as a tangible monetary investment, which a prudent worker would not drop lightly. In this period government did not provide unemployment benefits, workers' compensation, social security benefits, or Medicare/Medicaid. Therefore, union members depended on their unions for much more than wages and work rules. Financial help for one's family during times of unemployment or sickness could make the difference between life and death. This approach to unionism in America was pioneered by Samuel Gompers and other leaders of the Cigar Makers' International Union and was supported by the founders of the United Association.

Local 189 did not at first require high dues and initiation fees, but by 1901 it raised dues from ten to thirty cents a week. The initiation fee to the local was increased to $25 to match the UA's standard fee and represented more than a week's salary for journeymen. Members received stamps when they paid dues, which they pasted in a blue book to show they were paid up. In return, the new union offered a benefit of $5 a week for up to thirteen weeks to those who were ill or injured. Five dollars was the equivalent of about one-quarter of a week's salary. In 1909 the local enacted a $50 death benefit. Local 216 offered a similar benefit. In 1903 Local 216's business agent, George Taylor, strongly endorsed the new system in a letter to the *UA Journal*:

> There was a reason for dues being high. Maybe the boys met in a room where an American mechanic (the king of labor, peer of any, the inferior of none) was not ashamed to meet his fellow, and a good hall costs something. And, again, perhaps that hall was lighted up, so you could distinguish a five from a six dollar bill. Gas costs, too, and then again, perhaps the local found it advantageous to employ a

business agent, and they draw salary, sometimes. But if they did all these things their dues had to be higher and when they did all these things I'll take a small bet that conditions were lots better and also that the boys paying their high dues were a more intelligent lot of mechanics than the men who were members of the crafts around them who were paying a lower rate of dues. . . . Boys, when you are paying a higher rate of dues it means that you are trying to do something for yourselves; it means a bettering of our conditions, a higher standard of life (and incidentally gives you a chance to buy an umbrella, it might rain someday you know).

As Taylor made clear, higher dues enabled the local to do more than simply offer benefits. In 1901, after it signed its first collective bargaining agreement, the union could afford to provide its business agent with a home phone. The local could lease a hall semipermanently—its first hall was at 31½ Broad Street—and furnish it with chairs, tables, and, in 1910, with a dozen cuspidors for tobacco-chewing members. By 1920 there was a water fountain. Interestingly, the largest single yearly expense in these early days was for Labor Day uniforms and badges to members—over $300 in 1903.

At least as important as dues and benefits was paid, full-time leadership. The business agent, first called the "walking delegate," was the union's most important paid leader. In the fragmented, highly competitive construction industry, with its multitude of contractors and subcontractors scattered over the city in dozens of job sites, a mobile (or walking) union officer was necessary to see that journeymen and their employers were living up to the agreement and respecting the craft's jurisdiction; he was also an organizer, authorized to enroll new members in the union. The walking delegate had to have the authority to "pull a job" should he be unable to resolve a difficulty through negotiation. The power vested in the walking delegate made him, early on, the most important figure in the union. He soon took on a variety of business functions and began to be known as the business agent.

The first business agent was elected in 1901 and represented and was paid by both Columbus locals. He was responsible not only for enforcing the agreement and reporting violations to the Local's board of directors but for enforcing union by-laws. He had to register apprentices and helpers, collect fines, and check up on new jobs to see that union men were being hired. In November 1907 the business agent's responsibilities were expanded to include the supervision of the first union hiring hall. He was instructed to keep a written list of all new jobs received from union contractors and to show the list to any member who requested it. All members laid off were to give their names to the business agent to be registered "so as the first man off to receive the first job, in case the first man does not want the job, it will go to the second man, and so on, down the line, until the job is filled." Employers were not obligated to use the hiring hall in this era, only to use union labor. Most members found employment directly from contractors. In 1919 the business agent was charged with being sure that each member had a journeyman plumbers' license.

The business agent, of course, was not the only officer in the union. Every six months each Columbus local elected a president, vice-president, recording secretary, financial secretary, treasurer, outside and inside sentry, and board of directors. The board of directors served as the executive branch, formulating policy and making critical decisions, which were then recommended to the general membership at the regular meeting. Once endorsed, policy was put into effect by the business agent. There was also an examining board, established in 1902, and several committees to assist the regular officers; of these the finance and entertainment committees were the most important.

Another element that bound together members of the local was perhaps the most crucial: the intangible spirit of brotherhood that animated members of the craft to hold fast not only to the union but to the union ideal. Union members of today may find it difficult to escape the belief that the feelings and convictions underlying unionism were somehow preordained and inevitable. Any of the founders of Local 189 could have told them differently. The plumbing craft existed in Columbus for over three-quarters of a century before plumbers established a viable union. During those years, craftsmen generally viewed themselves as individuals trying to better themselves within the marketplace, hoping ultimately to become independent masters. Through the first two decades of this century the goal of becoming a contractor persisted, but unionism required that such individualism, though not abandoned, be tempered by a realization that the cooperation of journeymen with each other was a surer and more effective route to the advancement of all. Such a realization grew slowly and often developed from the experience of being exploited on the job, finding oneself on the street for standing up for one's rights, or participation in job actions and strikes. It also came simply from the experience of being part of the union and witnessing its advantages.

Unfortunately, historical records give only the vaguest impression of what brotherhood meant to the average union plumber and pipefitter. But there are tangible indications of how the union fostered this spirit. Unlike unions outside of the crafts, members of the United Association were elected to membership. Union membership, therefore, was something of a privilege. Indeed, with the closed shop, nonunion workers did not work at all. After proving themselves competent craftsmen either by passing through an apprenticeship or by being employed as journeymen for a like number of years, applicants took an examination administered by the union. After passing it, they were voted upon by the entire membership. Each member dropped a white ball or a black ball into a box, and if the majority of the balls were white, the applicant was accepted. It was rare but not unheard-of for an applicant recommended by the examining board to be rejected. Once voted into the union, the applicant took a solemn oath of loyalty to both the union and its members: to protect them in distress, to stand by them in time of strike, to help them procure employment.

Brotherhood was also evidenced by the sick committee, which visited members in distress and recommended payment of benefits for the needy. In the early days the union loaned up to $25 to out-of-work members upon recommendation by the board of directors. In one instance the local voted to assess itself $100 to send a brother afflicted with rheumatism to an area with hot springs.

Members regularly engaged in other rituals: the president's admonition to the sentries to remove all those who were not members (a protection against agents of the contractors), the past president's recitation of the purpose of the union at the start of each meeting, making the secret sign, draping the insignia of the union in black at the death of a brother, and the report of the sick committee as the first order of business at each meeting. Such rituals, which resembled and were partially based on those of centuries-old fraternal orders such as the Masons and had been adapted to labor purposes by the Knights of Labor, might seem silly or evidence of sheeplike thinking to an outsider. But rituals served an important purpose. They provided a means of drawing a sharp line in the unionist's mind between members and nonmembers and setting off the time spent on union business from time spent on everyday affairs. Their fellow members and everything they did during that time took on a special meaning that bound them together—much like the symbolic chain that links and encircles the UA emblem.

For this reason the local considered attendance at meetings a high priority and fined those who did not attend. Two years after its founding, the union raised the fine for nonattendance from ten to twenty-five cents, almost an hour's wage; later the fine was rescinded. Local minutes indicate that considerable time was taken up at many meetings discussing who was to be excused from the fine and whether to raise the fine for nonattendance. Thus in 1903 aged members were required to attend only one meeting out of the average of four each month. Throughout the first decade of Local 189's history there was debate over raising the fine for missing meetings to fifty cents and to a dollar for missing special meetings; some even advocated suspension. Despite these penalties, the attendance at early meetings ranged from 30 to 50 percent, though a large majority attended special meetings for elections and strike votes. For example, in 1903, fifty-two out of eighty-five members of Local 189 attended a nomination meeting. Weekly meetings were held until October 1926.

Another regular union gathering, stretching back to the founding of Local 57, was the annual and sometimes semiannual party or "blow-out" or "smoker," as it was called at the turn of the century. A menu for a 1905 banquet held by the fitters went as follows:

> Boiled Ham in Sandwich.
> Baked Beans with Pork.
> Smoked Sausage with Kraut.
> Potato Salad a la German.
> Cheese (on the Square).   Pickles, Slaw and Celery.
> Refreshments.
> Burs Paps.   Butter Milk.
> Sweet Milk.
> Cigars.

The affair included speeches, singing by business agent Al Seddon, and stories and jokes. According to the account, "The boys were having such a good time that it ran way into the small hours of the night before we adjourned."

Together with the spirit of brotherhood went a sense of male camaraderie expressed in hard drinking, mutual kidding and joking, and appreciation of hard-nosed, tough, and colorful characters. One of the earliest of the latter was the beloved J. W. Leonard, first president of Local 216, known to his friends as "Bill Nye." Leonard, a hard-drinking bachelor, had a reputation for always wearing dirty work clothes. In 1904 his fellow members kidded him in the *UA Journal* for

A Local 189 outing, 1916.

opposing a motion, which was eventually passed, that members dress in white
suits for Labor Day. For that occasion the following poem was dedicated to him:

Bill Nye on Parade

It was a bright September day,
And 'twas a glorious sight,
For there in Labor's grand parade,
Marched Bill Nye dressed in white.

The people voted this parade
The finest ever seen,
And towering far above the rest
Was our Bill Nye, and clean

The marchers stepped their liveliest,
The crowds were well behaved,

But 'tis not much to wonder at,
For our Bill Nye was shaved.

The band was playing stirring airs,
And how the crowd did holler,
The cause for this is very plain,
Our Bill Nye wore a collar.

The fair ones gazed in wonderment,
And many heaved a sigh,
For it doesn't often happen
That Bill puts on a tie.

But Bill marched on quite unconcerned
He didn't have a care,
And when he raised his cap 'twas seen,
He'd tried to part his hair.

But Labor Day has passed along
The memory's with us still,
Our uniforms are dirty now,
And so is dear old Bill.

If I were worth a million,
I'd bet it all to ten,
'Twill be a hundred thousand years
Till Bill cleans up again.

The strong sense of fraternity among the Columbus men of the pipe trades extended to the relations between Locals 189 and 216. On the national level, however, there was bitter jurisdictional rivalry between plumbers and pipefitters. To those outside the building trades incessant jurisdictional squabbling seems subversive of labor solidarity and the issues remote and often trivial. But to those involved, jurisdiction reflected the attempt to preserve a craft and one's livelihood. There were two major reasons for jurisdictional disputes within the pipefitting trade. First, because of technological changes that diminished the importance of

Brother J. W. Leonard, better known as "Bill Nye."

plumbers' leadworking skill, they began to be trained in the methods used by steamfitters. On many jobs that involved new technology, such as hooking up ice machines, the work could be and was done by either type of worker. The second reason was the existence of the International Association of Steam and Hot Water Fitters and Helpers (IA). Because the UA claimed jurisdiction over both plumbing and steamfitting work, it considered the IA a dual union and therefore illegitimate.

Numerous attempts by the American Federation of Labor to patch up the quarrel between the two organizations or to effect a merger failed in the first decade of the century. By 1911, the UA took the offensive and used its alliances with local contractors and building trades councils to pressure IA locals to switch affiliations. Many large projects were shut down when UA members walked off the job rather than work alongside IA members. In Boston, St. Louis, and Chicago the struggle turned bitter and violent. In Chicago "sluggers" were employed by both sides, resulting in numerous shootings and one death. One unfortunate consequence was that the UA lost standing in the labor movement, and the entire labor movement bore the onus of the frequent shutdowns and jurisdictional violence with which the public had no sympathy. Meanwhile, many IA locals either merged with UA locals or joined the UA as new locals. The big city locals joined after an AFL decision favoring the UA. By 1914, the IA ended its existence by merging with the UA.

Because there were no IA locals in Columbus, relations between fitters and plumbers were generally amicable. In 1903 Columbus fitter G. C. Tanant affirmed the value of fitters being in the same organization as plumbers: "It is beneficial to all alike, because it creates a better feeling among ourselves and enables us to adjust any differences that exist or occur in our branch of the trade in perfect harmony. . . . We have found the plumber ready at all times and perfectly willing to render all the assistance in their power to enable us to adjust any trouble that has or may occur in any of the shops in Columbus whenever any boss tries to infringe on our rules."

In the early years the locals shared not only the same recording secretary but the same business agent whom they jointly instructed. This was a highly unusual situation for two fitter and plumber locals, even though both were in the UA. And they met in the same hall on different days of the week. When negotiating with employers, the two locals set up a joint grievance committee that reported to a special joint meeting. Nonetheless, a friendly rivalry existed between the two locals, reflected in the plumbers' reference to fitters as "greasy-bellies" (for the grease on their overalls) and their half-joking definition of a fitter as "a plumber with his brains knocked out"; the fitters were only too glad to return the favor when defining the qualifications of a plumber: "Lacking brains isn't always necessary for the job, but it sure helps."

Jurisdictional disputes did occur in Columbus. As early as 1901 Local 189 considered charges from 216 that a plumber had installed a hot water fitting and decided to fine the member. Many disputes were headed off by a rule that plumbers and fitters could do each other's work as long as a job did not last longer than eight hours. But disputes continued, especially over new ice machine hookups and brewery work. The most divisive dispute took place in 1909 over who would control installation of vacuum cleaning systems. A board of directors report that year recommended "that if the members of 216 go ahead with this vacuum work, Local 189 will set the other crafts loose." Ultimately the conflict was resolved by a joint committee from both locals.

Though the 1913 national jurisdiction agreement with the IA that defined fitter and plumber work caused many plumber locals to grumble that the UA gave away too much, disputes decreased markedly by the 1920s. Nonetheless, internal jurisdictional tensions continued to plague the local until the post–World War II era, when work became plentiful for all.

Local Collective Bargaining

The exclusive agreement of May 6, 1901, at first seemed to promise a settlement to the incessant disputes between journeymen and masters since 1892. In 1902, for the first time, the union registered senior apprentices and helpers, issuing them working cards. As the local's minutes put it, "Our object in registering senior apprentices is to keep a record of how many are working and how long at the trade."

But problems quickly emerged that threatened to destroy the partnership with the employers in its infancy. In 1902 a master plumber continued to employ a journeyman who had been suspended from the union for failure to pay back a loan to the local. Meanwhile, the local requested a wage increase from the Master Plumbers' Organization. On March 28, after unsatisfactory negotiations, Locals 189 and 216 struck, charging that the MPA was violating the agreement. One journeyman described the joint meeting that decided to strike: "On the motion of Bro. Jack Leonhart [sic] the boys secured a good, dry basement and stored every tool that could be found and the key was turned over to the lockout committee. It was a grand sight on the night of March 26 to see the boys with their junk, some on dump wagons and some hiking with all kinds of tool receptacles to the rendevous [sic]. The scheme was a great success and had a big effect."

Nevertheless, the strike dragged on. After mediation by the State Arbitration of Ohio Board failed, the masters imported more than 30 nonunion plumbers and pipefitters but were unable to defeat the union. Only 8 of the 143 union members scabbed. After four weeks on the street, arbitration by a local judge restored the status quo with several important changes. The two locals won a twenty-five-cent increase for 1902 and another twenty-five-cent increase effective in 1903. Several concessions were also made regarding helpers. Locals 189 and 216 levied severe fines of $150 to $200 on the journeymen who scabbed—they were later reduced— and printed their names in the *UA Journal,* but there seems to have been no lasting ill feeling against the bosses. The *Dispatch* reported that "the friendly feeling that has marked the conduct of this struggle was carried into the settlement and the men return to their old places in the best possible spirit."

But trouble did not take long to recur. In March 1904, with the contract about to expire, Local 189 made a series of proposals to change it radically. First, the plumbers asked for a 50-cent wage increase to $3.50 a day, and fitters in Local 216 asked for $3.00, up from $2.75. That increase in the standard minimum wage was intended to equalize the wage between the less-skilled and more skilled mechanics, whom the bosses had been paying premiums of $1.00 to $2.00 a day. Second, both unions demanded that no new apprentices be hired, thus phasing out the apprenticeship program. Third, but no less important, the locals wanted to rescind the clause in the exclusive agreement that bound them to work only for MPA contractors. This blow at the contractors' monopoly may have been the major reason why the MPA refused to accept the demands of the union.

The contractors rejected the wage increases, stating that if they were granted, the amount paid to better mechanics would have to be raised proportionally by the increment in the minimum rate. The MPA also declared its determination to keep the apprenticeship ratio at 1:3, retain the exclusive agreement, and employ fitters and plumbers interchangeably during rush periods. The bosses threatened that if the union abrogated the exclusive agreement, they would adopt the open shop, which had already been established in Cincinnati and Dayton. Thus the stage was set for an all-out battle, the most protracted and bitter in the history of collective bargaining relations in the Columbus pipe trades. The looming conflict was particularly ironic because among the leaders of the MPA were former unionists who had had gone into business for themselves, including some of the founders of old Local 57. Among them were newly minted contractors Louis Bauman and Martin Stai.

The strike began in the last week of April 1904. During the first two weeks, while both sides searched for a settlement that would preserve the "combine," as the press called the exclusive agreement, the union made no attempt to work for nonassociation contractors nor did employers hire scabs. But on May 10, when the state of Ohio's Board of Arbitration stepped into the fray, the MPA refused to take part in conciliation proceedings, declaring in a public statement that it had decided to adopt the open shop: "This association will not in any manner meet with the union or their representatives. We have repeatedly decided without a single dissension that we will not settle with the unions but with the men as individuals, and that we intend to operate absolutely open shops." The employers began to import strikebreakers from other cities. By May 18 plumbers were being brought in at a rate of six to eight per day.

The union response was twofold. First, it decided to offer its members' services at the new scale to nonassociation contractors, generally smaller firms, in competition with the larger association firms. When this tactic did not generate enough work, the union formed its own cooperative plumbing and heating firm. Producers' cooperatives had been a popular ideal of the Knights of Labor in the 1880s. Master Workman Terence V. Powderly thought that worker-owned companies would eventually displace capitalism and enable workers to escape wage slavery. Though the founders of the American Federation of Labor favored incremental improvements through collective bargaining, the practice of forming cooperatives was familiar to plumbers and pipefitters, many of whose local unions had experience with them. The second approach to union journeymen was more direct: to do what they could to prevent scabs from taking their jobs, by persuasion if possible, by force if necessary.

Three days after the MPA's declaration regarding the open shop, the Hoffman-Conklin Plumbing Company secured a blanket court injunction prohibiting acts that union men had long assumed were their rights as citizens. Fifty union members were prohibited from picketing in front or in back of the firm's premises, from uttering threats to scabs, and from following them home. Local 189 was prohibited from fining or suspending those of its members who were scabbing or doing anything that would prevent them from working. Similar injunctions were issued on behalf of other contractors. By the end of the month J. W. Leonard and Tom Birch were brought before a local judge on contempt charges for threatening a strikebreaker.

Unable to picket, union members hoped to sell their labor to nonassociation contractors or go into business on their own. But the bosses had the support of the large builders, who refused to let contracts to anyone outside the association. Union men were left with a tiny field of work over which they increasingly squabbled among themselves. On July 19, 1904, the *Dispatch* reported the failure of the Cooperative Plumbing Company. Not only were capitalists conspiring to deprive it of business, but so many union members had opened small shops that no single shop, including the union shop, could make enough to meet costs. Even worse, those who were working often did not contribute to the support of those out of work, and by June this was a sore point within the union. By the end of the month many members were leaving town to find work. A final factor militating against the union was that the Building Trades Council was virtually dead, while the boss plumbers had the support of a strong citywide contractors' association as well as the city's leading businessmen. Though the city inspector charged in his official report that the MPA, using scab labor, had violated virtually every law in the city code, no action was taken against the powerful contractors.

The strike limped on into August, when it was called off. Though there is no written record of the exact events, the MPA ultimately abandoned the open shop, probably because it could not secure an adequate supply of skilled labor, and resumed collective bargaining by 1905. But its relationship with the union changed in that the latter restrained demands that might provoke conflict.

As in Columbus, union power ebbed and flowed throughout the country. Between 1901 and 1904 Columbus journeymen had steadily increased in numbers and power and had escalated their demands designed to seal off the market for labor in the trade. In the postdepression years from 1897 to 1903 the American labor movement had similar success, and the AFL quadrupled its membership. Still, despite the willingness of political reformers labeled Progressives to recognize collective bargaining, most employers refused to accept limits on their property rights. Beginning in 1902, employers, led by the militant National Association of Manufacturers, countered rising union power by reasserting the open shop.

Local businessmen and antiunion professionals organized citizens' industrial associations and used any and all methods to crush the labor movement. As a price of employment, workers were required to sign "yellow dog" contracts that bound them not to join a union. Companies spied on union activists and often fired them summarily; once out of work, they were blacklisted. Perhaps the most potent antiunion weapon was the court injunction—such as the one secured by Hoffman-Conklin Plumbing Company during the 1904 strike—which made it practically illegal to conduct most normal union activities. Between 1902 and 1916 the courts held that labor boycotts were illegal and sentenced AFL President Samuel Gompers to prison—the sentence was later overturned—for placing a firm on a "We Don't Patronize" list. Blanket injunctions prohibiting union members from exercising free speech during strikes, like the one issued against Local 189 in 1904, were also common. The American labor movement was fighting for its life during the decade after 1904.

Columbus, with its native-born, "all-American" labor force and weak union tradition, was a hospitable environment for the open-shop movement. The MPA's counterassault on Locals 189 and 216 in 1904 began a period of intense labor conflict in the Columbus area that ultimately destroyed many local unions. Though collective bargaining resumed in the pipe trades, it was conducted largely on the employers' terms for many years. Following the 1904 defeat, nonunion workmen were abundant in formerly union shops, and the closed shop became a dead letter. In July 1905 in a special meeting of Local 189 a committee of eighteen was appointed "for the purpose of building up the Local and getting outside plumbers to join." A smaller delegation was instructed to visit nonunion men, including those who had scabbed during the strike, and try to induce them to join the union for a lowered initiation fee of $10. Finally, the meeting called on "each brother to be a committee of one to see the scabs in each shop." Within the next two months twenty-one new applications were accepted, and the union soon regained much of its former strength. By 1906 the union was able to formulate and enforce a new set of working rules, which included an eight-hour workday for $3 and time and a half for overtime.

Yet other demands that had been raised in 1904 were not pressed. Apprentices remained, as did helpers. In 1907 members preferred charges in the local against plumbers using unregistered helpers, and the local resolved that "we keep what we have and not register any more." Nevertheless, the helpers remained. Perhaps the most important test of the union's new approach to collective bargaining was its unwillingness to use the strike to press its concerns. For twenty-two years following the 1904 strike, neither of the two locals resorted to a walkout to gain its demands.

In 1907 and 1908 the union faced a renewed problem of unemployment because of a national depression. In Columbus growth in employment was slow until World War I began in 1914. During these years many members went into business for themselves, increasing the competition for scarce work. Most formed small shops employing only themselves and no other journeymen, thereby decreasing employment opportunities for union journeymen. In April 1909 the local passed a rule that these members not be given withdrawal cards, thus continuing to subject them to union rules.

Meanwhile, the labor movement in Columbus reached a high point with the attempt to unionize the city's streetcar company. The resulting streetcar strike was the most bitter and bloody in the history of the city up to that time. Much of the city's sympathy was on labor's side, and large crowds from the working-class neighborhoods of Steelton in the far south and Flytown and the Milo-Grogan district north of downtown attacked streetcars driven by heavily armed scabs. About one-quarter of the police force refused to obey orders to ride on the cars, in effect mutinying. The police were outraged that the mayor had just vetoed a bill for an eight-hour day for police officers but signed one granting himself a salary increase. Rock- and brick-throwing and then dynamiting of cars intensified tensions in the city and brought in the National Guard. At the end of the strike, Columbus's working people protested by voting Socialist in record numbers—30 percent of the vote—in 1910. Four members of the Socialist party were elected to the City Council and two to the Board of Education.

Until the start of war in Europe in 1914, the plumbers and steamfitters did not press for major improvements in their contracts but rather continued to guard existing wage rates and work rules. One of the main reasons was the antiunion atmosphere in Columbus. In 1916, for example, the state organizer for the Ohio Building Trades Council reported that "conditions in Columbus are becoming so bad the Chief of Police is ordering organizers out of town, subjecting them to the Third Degree." Police arrested the organizer in question, along with the president of the Columbus Federation of Labor, for addressing a noon organizing meeting at a local manufacturing plant.

Another time the assistant mayor called a dozen building trades union organizers along with union machinists into his office and told them to get out of town. They were loaded into a patrol wagon and dumped at the city limits. When a mass protest meeting was held at which AFL president Samuel Gompers was scheduled to speak, the chief of police made a public boast—which he failed to carry out—that he would personally prevent Gompers from speaking.

In 1919 the state Building Trades Council decided against meeting in Columbus. As one delegate put it: "That city is positively dominated by the manufacturing associations. Every cent spent in Columbus will be taken in a spirit to be used against us."

Two World Wars and the Great Depression

In April 1917, after three years of neutrality, the United States entered the Great War on the side of the Allies. In this war "to make the world safe for democracy," Columbus plumbers and pipefitters rallied to the government's call to arms.

Following the lead of the AFL's Gompers, UA general president John Alpine pledged to avoid strikes on government work and disassociated the UA from the Socialists and other dissenters in the labor movement who opposed involvement in the conflict and led a wave of strikes in 1917. In return for labor's pledge of support, the federal government, under President Woodrow Wilson, backed many of labor's demands: recognition of existing collective bargaining agreements, the right of workers in war-related industries to organize, the eight-hour day, and equal pay for equal work for women. The trade union movement expanded greatly, and the UA increased its membership by 50 percent nationwide between 1917 and 1920. Local 189 grew to close to two hundred members by the early 1920s.

During the war, Columbus citizens took pride in a local boy, Eddie Rickenbacker, who became the country's foremost flying ace, and they sacrificed by doing without fuel every Monday. Local 189 demonstrated its patriotism by subscribing to two $2,000 Liberty Loan bond issues. Among the members of the local who served in the armed forces, two lost their lives: William Gleich and Lester Link. Louis Bauman, who had rejoined the local as a journeyman, was so enthusiastic and patriotic that he often waited at the train station to offer servicemen without a room the use of his family's home.

In addition to eliciting patriotic sacrifice, the war led to economic developments that created both opportunities and dangers for union members. With the prolific distribution of government contracts, industrial construction surged in Columbus. By early 1918 fifty area firms were engaged in war production; employment was further augmented by the erection of a $7 million government storage depot and a series of nearby cantonments (military training facilities). But residential construction declined so many plumbers and pipefitters were still not assured of adequate employment. Those fortunate enough to have government jobs worked many overtime hours, but others worked irregularly. In July 1918 the local voted narrowly to assess all those working on the federal storage depot a $2 a month tax.

A still greater problem was the rising cost of living. Held in check during the war, prices soared after the Armistice in November 1918. By 1919, workers all over America, including the more than one million newly organized during the war, were striking for wages that would enable them to keep up with rising prices. In Columbus there was no strike wave although workers were concerned about inflation. In August two charter members of the local, Mike Ginley and

Louis Bauman, led a union committee that called for federal regulation of the meat-packing industry to halt its monopolistic pricing policies. According to the resolution passed at the meeting, Local 189 "deem[s] it necessary to reduce the cost of living at this time and whereas the condition of the laboring people is becoming intolerable . . . we must have some immediate relief." At the same meeting the local decided to buy government surplus food to sell to members at cost.

In October a joint committee of Locals 189 and 216 demanded an increase in wages from approximately $.60 per hour to $1 but quickly settled for an increase to $.90 in 1920 in a contract that was to last until 1922. Contrary to expectations, the cost of living continued to rise. In May 1920 UA general organizer Charles Dickson arrived in Columbus to find that both locals were about to go on strike for a further wage increase to $1.25. At a special joint meeting, at Dickson's urging, the men voted 104 to 73 to rescind their strike call and honor the agreement.

In 1920 the inflationary spiral of the postwar years suddenly came to an end and prices fell sharply. In the nation's major industrial areas employers, led by the U.S. Chamber of Commerce and National Association of Manufacturers, launched a counterattack on the labor movement with a newly invigorated open-shop movement, which they dubbed the "American Plan." In former union strongholds such as San Francisco, Minneapolis–St. Paul, and Chicago, large manufacturers successfully imposed the open shop, at least for several years, on the smaller and less cohesive construction industry contractors. In Cleveland and in most areas of the country the UA was on the defensive. In vain the *UA Journal* editorialized in 1920: "Unionism means Americanism, Non-Unionism means Feudalism."

Columbus was an exception to this trend. There was no open-shop movement in that city because unionism was weak in most trades. In the pipe trades the long-standing friendly relations between the MPA and the two UA locals prevented employers from pushing for an open shop. In January 1921 general organizer Dickson reported that "the affairs of our locals in Columbus are in good shape, and the other trades will have to help themselves, or at least show some effort to do so prior to our locals placing themselves on the altar of sacrifice." In 1922 the contractors signed a new two-year agreement raising wages from $.90 to $1 an hour, or $8 a day, at a time when many other UA locals were fighting wage cuts. The following spring, when it became clear that the city's new building boom would continue, employers voluntarily raised the wage another $1 a day. "Our Plumbers and Steam Fitters Local Unions are in a far better condition than any of the other building trades of the city," boasted Dickson in the fall of 1923.

The decade of the 1920s was one of prosperity for the city, but the benefits of that prosperity were unevenly distributed. Poorly organized industrial workers and blacks were left behind. In downtown Columbus the Civic Center and the American Insurance Union building (Lincoln-LeVecque Tower), Port Columbus airport, Ohio Stadium on the university campus, and Beulah Park were built and Bexley emerged as an exclusive suburban city. The Timken Company and Ford Motor Company built plants in the city offering good jobs for union construction workers. For plumbers and pipefitters the prosperity and good feeling during this construction boom was punctuated only by a short strike in June 1926, which resulted in a pay increase for the city's three hundred plumbers and pipefitters to $11 a day. That year the union decided not to demand that the five-and-a-half-day week be cut to five days or that all overtime be paid at double-time rates.

Progress in the 1920s occurred through negotiated settlements and friendly cooperation with the contractors, most notably in the area of apprenticeship. Until the 1920s America's need for skilled labor was filled primarily by immigrants. The end of unrestricted immigration in 1921 and 1924 followed by the building boom of the early 1920s made employers recognize the need for new ways to train skilled journeymen in America. Unionists also began to accept the necessity for more formalized systems of training. Previously, unionists had favored regulation of apprenticeship to restrict entry into the trade so as to maintain standard minimum wages and working conditions. When advocates of the open shop began training programs and the demand for labor boomed, making an oversupply seem remote, the UA began to emphasize the training aspect of apprenticeship as well as the restrictive aspect. In Chicago the fitters' union abolished the helper category and instituted an apprenticeship program under the auspices of a joint board of unionists and employers in cooperation with the city's Board of Education, which sponsored classes one day every other week. In 1922 the UA convention established a five-year apprenticeship program.

That same year Local 189 established its own apprenticeship training program in cooperation with the Columbus public school system. By 1927 apprenticeship training had become part of an Ohio-wide program authorized by the State Board of Vocational Education and State Joint Apprenticeship Commission. Apprentices were paid by employers for four hours each week spent in school and attended

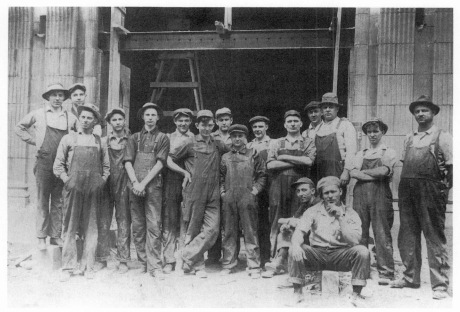

*Plumbers and pipefitters pose at the foot of
LeVecque Tower, completed in 1927.*

school through four years of apprenticeship. In 1927 Local 189 nominated Francis
Graham to attend an apprenticeship training course for instructors at Pittsburgh's
Carnegie Institute of Technology while serving as plumbing school director. Later
in the year another local official, Arthur M. Barr, attended a two-week intensive
training program held at Ohio State University. This program went out of
existence when the Great Depression hit the country in 1929.

Another area in which contractors and the union cooperated was in enforcing
state and city plumbing and steamfitting codes. Both parties had an interest in
doing so to prevent the skilled labor employed by the contractors from being
undercut by lower-paid, often shoddy, nonunion work. Throughout the decade,
aggressive open-shop forces attempted to dilute the state code in the legislature
and before the Board of Building Standards. "There has been a well defined plan
formulated in this State," wrote general organizer Dickson in 1928, "to tear down
all our state, county, and city plumbing laws which are for the protection of public
health, as well as a protection to our industry." Like earlier efforts, this plan was
beaten back by an industrywide coalition of contractors and unionists.

The era of cooperation lasted until 1927, when the building boom began to taper off. Even before the Great Depression sparked by the stock market crash of October 1929, the construction industry was in decline. In January 1929 a joint meeting of Locals 189 and 216 reported that "the plumbing and steamfitting industry in Columbus has been deteriorating for the last two years. The nonunion shop and nonunion journeymen are securing a good percentage of the work that was formerly done by our employers and our members." The same month Local 189 recommended that Locals 189 and 216 merge to save salary costs and to unify forces to defend against expected efforts by the contractors to impose a wage cut. The merger plan protected the interests of the fitters, who would be outnumbered, by mandating that the board of directors be composed of the three plumbers and three fitters receiving the highest number of votes.

That same year marked another milestone for Local 189. Tom Birch, who had served as business agent since 1908 and had helped orchestrate much of the cooperation with the MPA, retired and was replaced by Arthur M. Barr.

The Great Depression did not hit the Columbus economy as hard as those of more industrial cities. Still, about a third of the work force was unemployed, and Local 189 was in a precarious position. In April 1930, when the contractors demanded a wage cut, a special meeting was held at which the attendees refused, for the first time, to give the negotiating committee a free hand to act on behalf of the local, authorizing it only to "stand pat for the old agreement." The contractors refused to accept this and offered a $2 a day—18 percent—reduction in pay along with a loss of travel pay inside of Franklin County. When the local rejected a new offer from the MPA on July 8 for a wage of $10 a day, the contractors locked out their journeymen. A week later, at an acrimonious meeting, the MPA's offer was accepted after nine and a half hours of discussion. The mood of the men was captured in the motion passed that the union "strictly enforce our working rules from now on" and suggest that the MPA adopt a five-day week to relieve unemployment.

The Great Depression hit no industry harder than construction. In Ohio the number of construction workers employed dropped by almost half between August 1929 and January 1930. By 1932 there were 66.8 percent fewer building trades workers in the state than in 1929. Wages fell correspondingly, from a yearly statewide average of $1,668 in 1929 to $982 in 1932, a drop of 41 percent. Local 189's membership figures understated the decline in work available in the pipe trades in Columbus, for many members paid dues even when they were not working in the hope that conditions would improve. In 1929 the merged local had 224 members, a decline from 1927, when together both locals had about 300 members. The number continued to decline: to 211 in 1930, 179 in 1931, 160 in 1932, 139 in 1933, reaching a low of 119 in 1936, a 60 percent decline from a decade earlier. Several members recalled that not more than a third of the local's membership had work through the mid-1930s.

In August 1930 the local's finance committee's recommendations that the union move to a cheaper hall, discontinue the practice of making personal loans, and require officers to pay dues from which they had previously been exempted were accepted. Only members working more than five days a month were required to pay dues. A motion to combine the offices of business agent, financial secretary, and treasurer was seriously discussed but rejected. In an attempt to restrict entry into the trade, the local quadrupled the initiation fee to $100.

In 1934 so many members had dropped out that the local decided to take them back for the regular initiation fee of $25 plus one year's back dues. It was a time marked by soup kitchens, destitute people selling apples on street corners, families losing their homes, and unemployed workers desperately competing for scarce work. Many worked intermittently and therefore ate and heated their homes intermittently.

The American labor movement abounded with ideas for spreading out the available work. The most popular among construction workers was the five-day, thirty-hour workweek endorsed by the AFL in 1930. In 1931 and again in 1934 the local discussed this matter with the MPA, but nothing came of it. Many construction unions established job rotation plans enforced through the union hiring hall, but this option was not considered by Local 189. In 1932 the local discussed whether to enforce a rule that members not work Saturdays and Sundays so as to increase the number of hours available for work-sharing, but the attempt was abandoned.

As the pressure to earn enough to maintain one's family grew more critical, longtime jurisdictional rivalry within the local resurfaced. Francis Wolfe recalled that plumbers and fitters quarreled frequently and often bitterly at union meetings. Loyalty to the union eroded. One member, who was a helper in the 1930s, remembered that helpers resisted the ambition to become journeymen and union members because that would almost surely mean getting laid off. Job work (individual contracting), taken on the sly by union men, was widely resorted to, and many others took nonunion jobs if nothing else was available. The most flagrant case was that of former president and business agent Arthur M. Barr, who was fined $25 in 1933 for working in an unfair shop. Many members, however, paid their dues and took pride in not crossing picket lines.

Loyalty to the union was tested in 1933, when the local entered the longest strike in its history after refusing to accept another pay cut requested by the MPA. When the MPA reduced pay unilaterally in June from $1 an hour to $.75, the local established a lockout committee, set up pickets, and assessed all working members $1 a day. After a month on strike, the local decided to collect regular strike assessments even from those not working. With so little work available, there was not much incentive to reach an agreement, and the strike dragged on into the fall. The $.96 wage agreement represented a hollow victory for a union most of whose members were out of work.

The election of Franklin Delano Roosevelt as president of the United States in November 1932 marked a turning point in the downward spiral of labor's fortunes. For one of the few times in American history a pro-labor administration was in power. Three important pieces of legislation of interest to construction workers preceded the New Deal. The Bacon-Davis Act of 1931 and an Ohio law of the same year mandated that the prevailing wage, defined as the wage resulting from collective bargaining agreements in the private sector, must be paid on federal, state, and locally assisted construction projects. These laws prevented government-run construction projects from undercutting the gains won by union journeymen in collective bargaining. In 1932 Congress passed the Norris-LaGuardia Act, which outlawed "yellow-dog" contracts and abolished the practice of federal judges issuing antilabor injunctions except in carefully defined circumstances.

The first major piece of New Deal legislation that promoted collective bargaining was the National Industrial Recovery Act (NIRA) of 1933. The law exempted industry from antitrust laws so it could regulate its own prices. In return, the government demanded in section 7(a) that firms allow their employees to bargain collectively through agents of their own choosing and that employees be protected by minimum wages and maximum hours established under a federal code. The NIRA sparked a minor revival of the labor movement, especially in mass production industries, but section 7(a) was too often ignored by industrialists, and the federal government lacked sufficient enforcement mechanisms.

In 1935, even before the U.S. Supreme Court declared the NIRA unconstitutional, Congress passed the National Labor Relations Act, popularly known as the Wagner Act, which reaffirmed section 7(a) but put teeth in it. The Wagner Act was a revolutionary reversal of national labor policy, for through it the federal government squarely supported the formation of unions without any concessions to management. The act defined unfair labor practices on the part of employers but imposed no restraints on unions. To enforce the law the federal government established the National Labor Relations Board (NLRB) with power to hold elections among a firm's employees to certify a bona fide union—company unions were outlawed—as an exclusive bargaining agent. Among its powers, the NLRB could hear workers' complaints about unfair labor practices by management and issue "cease and desist" orders. With passage of the Fair Labor Standards Act of 1938, establishing a minimum wage and the eight-hour day and outlawing child labor, an array of legal protections backing the right of American workers to organize and bargain collectively were in place.

But legal protection for unionism meant little if workers had no jobs. The Great Depression had shaken an entire generation's faith in the ability of corporate leaders to provide economic prosperity and job security. It was particularly disillusioning to highly skilled construction workers like the plumbers and pipefitters, who had traditionally rejected the union goal of guaranteed employment and instead relied on their individual skills as mechanics to win work. The shock of long-term unemployment and impoverishment led most Local 189 members to welcome the New Deal's intervention in the economy to provide jobs, especially when the alternative was charity or welfare. Initially, the federal government's Civil Works Administration (CWA) and the Public Works Administration (PWA) provided jobs on public construction for building tradesmen. More important was the Works Progress Administration (WPA) begun in 1935.

The PWA and WPA had important repercussions for construction workers, for government work quickly overshadowed private sector employment during the New Deal. Although plumbers and pipefitters were grateful that they could retain their self-respect by earning their living through labor rather than resorting to welfare, they were ambivalent about direct government employment. Some provisions of the WPA, in particular, were threatening to Local 189 members, a large proportion of whom worked for the WPA by the late 1930s for $36 every two weeks. By allowing nonunion men to work in construction and by paying all workers a "security wage," which was lower than the union scale, the WPA undermined long-standing collective bargaining agreements reached in the private sector. Ultimately, the government and the union resolved this dispute by reducing the number of hours unionized construction workers were required to work to gain their security wage, thus maintaining the private sector wage.

The 1930s was a time of great progress for the labor movement in American society. But within the house of labor, turmoil and upheaval reigned. The industrial unions seceded from the AFL in 1935, and in 1938 the Congress of Industrial Organizations (CIO) was established independent of the AFL. The CIO did a great service for American workers by organizing the mass production sector of the economy that had been a bastion of the open shop since the failure of the Knights of Labor in the late nineteenth century. But for craft unions such as the plumbers and pipefitters, the CIO appeared as a threat, partly because of bitter personal rivalry between the AFL's William Green and the CIO's John L. Lewis, partly because of the radical political affiliations of many CIO organizers and leaders, but mostly because the CIO would submerge craft identities within industrial unions, for example having a single union for the construction industry. Though such a union never became a serious competitor to the building trades unions, the threatened competition and the example of the CIO's organizing success quickly galvanized the stodgy AFL craft unions into inaugurating rival organizing campaigns.

In 1937 the UA directed locals to organize their jurisdictions fully, including the growing field of refrigeration, take apprentices into the union, and even bring into membership "all those in wholesale houses, great and small that handle our materials, who must be organized into auxiliaries or unions of their own. . . . If this is not done, someone else will do it for us and when they do, then we will lose not only control of our materials and mechanical installation, but will lose complete control of our destiny as well." UA general secretary-treasurer Thomas Burke criticized many locals for operating in a "non-progressive" manner out of the fear "that if they organize a great many men in their own local union, it may destroy the opportunity for work for themselves, which is a very false delusion."

As UA locals took that criticism to heart, UA national membership, which had plummeted to less than thirty-five thousand in 1935, began to rise, reaching fifty-four thousand in 1938. In Columbus membership revived as well. By January 1937 so many new men were joining that the local hotly debated a motion that no more applications be accepted for ninety days before defeating it. In 1938 the local took in refrigeration men as an auxiliary body. The local also went on record in favor of allowing helpers to join the union, though other evidence indicates that few if any were actually allowed into the organization before World War II.

In 1937, after Congress established the Apprenticeship Training Service (now the Bureau of Apprenticeship and Training), the UA allowed its local unions to admit apprentices to membership following a probationary period. Local 189 set up its own apprenticeship committee, but lack of funding delayed an ongoing apprenticeship program until after the war. Though in 1940 the U.S. census listed sixteen apprentices in Columbus, they were not being trained formally.

Altogether, between 1936 and 1939 membership in Local 189 increased 55 percent. The strengthened organization decided in 1937 to ask for a large wage increase, and the MPA conceded an increase to $1.375 an hour without a strike.

By 1939 construction was in the beginning stages of a major boom, mainly in industrial and government work as a result of the start of a new European war and the decision of Congress to rearm. Thus, even before the entry of the United States into World War II on December 7, 1941, following the Japanese attack on the American naval base at Pearl Harbor, American construction workers were enjoying full employment. By 1941 members of Local 189 were helping to build the army air base at Lockbourne, Wright-Patterson Air Base in Dayton, the Marion Ordnance Plant and Depot, the Ravenna Ordnance Plant, and the Army Service Forces Depot in Columbus. More important than any of these projects for local members was the beginning of construction in 1941 in Columbus of the huge Curtis Wright airplane factory, which at its wartime peak employed twenty-six thousand workers. Unfortunately, much of the city was deteriorating because of the diversion of scarce materials and labor to the war effort. Racketeering, prostitution, gambling, and a large municipal debt plagued Columbus. These were big issues when young James Allen Rhodes was elected mayor on the Republican ticket in 1943. He would later serve four terms as governor of the state.

The union enjoyed prosperity as its membership soared from 184 in 1939 to 335 in 1943 during the peak of wartime production. Two important developments within the trade occurred as a result of the unprecedented demand for labor that had lasting effects on the local. First, helpers were brought into the union as journeymen for the first time when the local could not meet the demand of Curtis Wright for mechanics. The local increased the allotment for apprentices and in 1942 seriously considered establishing an apprenticeship school. In the late 1940s laborers "in the ditch" would also be brought into the union. But not enough new journeymen were added to avoid a serious undersupply of labor.

In the second development, contractors met this demand for journeymen by hiring nonunion mechanics. During the war the employment of these men in commercial and industrial work—they had always been a majority in residential plumbing—led to a serious erosion of craft standards. Union officials complained constantly during the war that the installation of plumbing in defense housing did not meet code standards. The formation of a pool of semiskilled nonunion mechanics would bring trouble to the union in the postwar period.

In 1941 the local found itself in an anomalous position with the Building Trades Council. For over thirty years the local generally had held itself aloof from the BTC, first as a result of its exclusive agreement with the MPA and, after the agreement was abandoned, as a result of the BTC's lack of effectiveness. In 1941 the Columbus BTC concluded an exclusive agreement with the Building Trades Employers Association of Columbus. This became a problem for Local 189 because several large nonunion contractors, employing a total of approximately one hundred men, received contracts from general contractors affiliated with the employers association. Because Local 189 was affiliated with the BTC, it was unable to organize these firms. In March 1942 the UA, which much earlier, after painful experience, had disavowed the concept of exclusive agreements, recommended that Local 189 disaffiliate from the BTC over this issue.

The union's general secretary-treasurer, Martin Durkin, wrote to general organizer Frank Schlenzig: "We agree . . . that the best cure for the non-union condition in Columbus is a vigorous campaign for the organization of the non-union workers, rather than trying to create a monopoly for some group of employers who enter into an agreement such as the one you have forwarded." After withdrawing from the BTC, the local signed an agreement with the MPA that afforded the plumbers and pipefitters an increase to $1.50 per hour, or $12.00 a day, an increase over the $1.375 they had gained in 1937. The five-day week, which had been won the previous year, remained in the agreement.

When war was declared, Local 189 performed its patriotic duty as it had during World War I. As UA policy dictated, the local kept up the dues of members who enlisted in the armed forces. By 1942 the local had also invested in $15,000 worth of defense bonds; members held another $4,500 worth. Local members donated hundreds of dollars each month for the benefit of their peers in the armed forces. At the front of the hall the union displayed a service flag bearing a blue star, the names of members in the service, and a gold star for those who were killed in the service of their country. Officers tried to live up to the pledge of AFL president William Green and UA president George Masterson that the union would forbear strikes so that the wartime effort would proceed uninterrupted. Union members were severely tested in keeping this pledge. Inflation continually outran the small increases in wages granted by the federal Wage Adjustment Board. Local 189 members received a total of eight cents per hour in raises over the war years. Frequent overtime and serious overwork on the job resulted in untold numbers of incidents. Still, the local carried out its pledge and did not strike.

The period from the late 1930s through the war years was a great watershed in the history of Local 189. After a third of a century as a small, conservative, nonmilitant organization, the local entered a golden era of full employment, explosive membership growth, and prosperity that would last until the late 1960s. Federal and state government commitment to the principles of collective bargaining, government sponsorship of union-employer apprenticeship training programs to supply manpower needs, and the belated acceptance of unionism by Columbus's city fathers allowed Local 189 to take advantage of the postwar boom to increase its size dramatically, improve wages and working conditions, establish an array of fringe benefits, and become more militant and progressive in its dealings with contractors. These developments also opened the way to renewed commitment to the principles of inclusiveness and labor solidarity and to fundamental changes in the character of Local 189.

4. Building a Stronger and Fairer Union, 1945–1973

At the end of World War II the daily work life and customs of the typical Local 189 member were in many ways little changed from the early years of the century. A majority of the members of the union, at least two-thirds, were plumbers, with steamfitters in a decided minority. The category of helper still existed, and apprenticeship training was largely informal. The union remained what it always had been: a closed corporation. If a young man had a father or a close relative, perhaps a friend, who was in the local, he might be able to join as an apprentice; otherwise his chances of becoming a plumber or pipefitter were slim. Both women and blacks were informally but effectively excluded. In 1950 there were twenty-two black plumbers and pipefitters actively working in Columbus, all outside the union, constituting approximately 2.5 percent of the active craftsmen in the city, both union and nonunion.

About three-quarters of Local 189's almost five hundred members worked out of six to eight large mechanical contractor shops in Columbus, among them Esswein, Huffman-Wolfe, Lieb-Jackson, Limbach, and Sauer. Most of the rest worked in two- to three-man shops, many doing residential construction and service work. On the job plumbers supplied all their caulking tools, which included a small pipe wrench, hammer, and joint runner (used for pouring lead). They also supplied their own ruler and pliers, as they still do. Steamfitters furnished only ruler and pliers. All else was supplied by the employer. Employers strongly emphasized working a full eight hours. Journeymen worked until 4:30 sharp, in contrast to today, when they use the last twenty minutes for cleaning up. The custom of taking a coffee break—not written into the rules—had begun on some jobs during and after the war but was not general practice until the early 1950s with the advent of the catering truck. Each journeyman brought his thermos from home, and sometime during the morning he would pour a cup of coffee.

According to contractual agreement, all firms paid in cash, not by check. Only social security was withheld. Many Local 189 members did not believe in checking accounts and did all their business with cash only. When pay increased and deductions for items such as health and welfare were added to the contract, employers switched to paying by check in the mid-1950s.

Compared to today's complex jobs, most work was simple and could be handled by the foreman. Few companies had large staffs. The foreman *was* the company on the job, and because the foreman was a union man, the company had little or no involvement in determining how work was conducted. A steamfitter was a steamfitter; he knew how to run his lines, hang his radiators, and hook up his pumps, and no one tried to tell him how to do his job. Technology was primitive compared to today. Refrigeration was limited to ice plants and cold storage plants. Control work was in its infancy. Process piping in factories did not require intricate control mechanisms. Traditional skills such as lead wiping were still widespread. Though welding had come in before and during the war years, the welders in the local were still a select group of journeymen in the 1940s. In short, the journeyman was not required to know much beyond what he picked up informally and haphazardly.

According to the 1950 U.S. census, Columbus plumbers and pipefitters (a category that encompassed those actively working at the trade both inside and outside the union) were not particularly young. Two-thirds were over thirty-five years old, and 43 percent were over forty-five. The year 1950 was relatively prosperous for the craft. Approximately two-thirds worked at least fifty weeks. Of those reporting income, two-thirds received more than the median income for the male civilian labor force in Columbus in 1950—$3,000. The median income for plumbers and pipefitters was $3,717.

The union was run loosely. The same person served as business manager and business agent. The agent rarely visited a job; he would learn about the employment conditions in his jurisdiction by asking members at meetings to fill out a card stating who they worked for and how many men were on the job. The hiring hall existed but lacked formal, mutually agreed-upon rules to guarantee fairness. A contractor who wanted to hire a particular journeyman would make arrangements directly with the man in question. Even members who used the hall did not benefit from the first-in, first-out rule. As a result, contractors could maintain an informal blacklist of members who might stand up for union rules on the job.

As they had before the war, local contractors continued to exercise a great deal of influence in the union behind the scenes, not only through their control of hiring but through their steady employees or "key men." Many of these men—though by no means all—were of divided loyalties. When contract proposals were voted on, they appeared "out of the woodwork" to vote as their employers wished. They would argue sincerely that the contractors could not accept certain proposals. Thus it was common for demands for ambitious contract provisions such as large pay increases and double time for overtime to be shelved at the last minute after contractors made it clear to their men that they would not accede to certain demands without a long strike.

Nonunion workers were largely limited to residential work, which was dominated by nonunion contractors. In the rest of the industry, members of Local 189 would not work on the job with nonunion men from any trade. This was a strict rule to which hardly any exceptions were made, and it reflected not only the union's control of commercial and industrial jobs but the solidarity of the building trades in Columbus immediately after the war (the union had rejoined the BTC). Through the mid-1960s if a contractor hired nonunion men of any craft, he was considered a nonunion or scab contractor and would lose his union work force. Because Local 189 members almost universally believed in direct action in that period, a nonunion contractor trying to crack the union's sphere was likely to find the heads of his scab employees cracked as well.

The union continued to be held together by its fraternal character. Union meetings and leisure activities were important in creating solidarity, but, like plumbers and pipefitters elsewhere, Local 189 members were also bound together by a shared language that reflected their shared job experiences. Thus plumbers never pronounced "caulking iron" according to the dictionary but called it "corking iron." A foreman who supervised too closely was known as a "bird dog" or was suspected of "trying to find out my shirt size." The tradition of walking off the job without union authorization, usually to protest an encroachment on the journeyman's jurisdiction, which in factories might be called a "wildcat," was known as a "wobble." A popular line of the time had it that while at work the journeyman's favorite topic of conversation was "liquor, women and OT [overtime]." The journeyman, especially the young one, might at times "pull a nooner," which was to start drinking at lunch and never return. A plumber or fitter fed up with his job might say, "I've got the red ass." When he quit the job for whatever reason, he would "pull the pin" (perhaps a carryover from the war) or "drag up." Occasionally, these terms were used outside the union, as when Local 189 member Pat Ferry, upon coming home to find his wife unexpectedly gone, heard his daughter offer the explanation: "Maybe mommy's drug up."

Plumbers, in particular, had (and still have) a wry sense of humor, referring to themselves as "honeydippers" or describing their work to laymen by saying "Your sh— is my bread and butter." In the days before welding, to cut a thread on a pipe was "to put a wrinkle (or a worm) on it." Plumbers and fitters distinguished themselves from other crafts by the slang names they gave the materials they used: "a bullheaded pipe" (the end that went into a "T") or "a gorilla welder" ("awful strong, awful ugly"—an incompetent welder). Language also expressed members' pride in their craft skill. A worker might be derisively described as having a "number 17 shirt and a number 2 hat," in short, that he was fit for the "bull gang" (heavy labor). The highest compliment a man could receive in the craft was the simple statement, "He's a good mechanic."

Language drew distinctions among Local 189 members as well as among crafts. One of the most enduring distinctions in the union was between the men called "steady Eddies," who worked steadily over an extended period of time for one contractor because they had become his "key men," and those who changed jobs relatively frequently, worked out of the hall, and hence were subject to spells of joblessness. Sometimes the latter group referred to themselves with belligerent pride as "hall trash." Both groups contained many strong union men, but those who were employed steadily liked to think of themselves first as "good mechanics" while those who changed jobs frequently had a stronger psychological dependence on the union, greater antipathy toward the boss, and liked to think of themselves first as "good union men." They attributed their lack of employment to their willingness to stand up for union rules on the job, not to any deficiencies in their mechanical skills.

As the early postwar years gave way to the booming 1950s and 1960s, large numbers of young journeyman with new concerns entered the union. As a result, the old distinction between those with and without steady jobs would become more important.

Technology and Apprenticeship

The late 1940s and 1950s began a period of accelerated industrial and technolog-ical change in the United States that greatly affected the division of work and the way it was carried on by UA journeyman. This was especially true in Columbus. Before the war the city's business leadership resisted large-scale industry, fearing that it would bring in strong unions. The establishment in Columbus of Curtis Wright (renamed North American Aviation, later Rockwell International) during the war changed all that. At its height, Curtis Wright employed twenty-six thousand workers, only five thousand fewer than were engaged in all manufactur-ing industries in prewar Columbus. In 1941 the United Auto Workers won an election at Curtis Wright allowing it to represent twelve thousand employees, at one stroke greatly increasing the numbers and political clout of the labor movement in Columbus.

The wartime industrial boom laid the groundwork for future expansion in the city. Columbus had the manpower, large tracts of inexpensive land, and the infrastructure to lure manufacturers. In the late 1940s and early 1950s Columbus experienced a major boom in manufacturing construction. General Motors and Timken Roller Bearing built new plants for the manufacture of auto and aviation equipment; they were joined by Westinghouse, which manufactured electrical machinery, and by numerous subcontractors, including foundries and manufactur-ers of heating and cooling equipment. To serve these factories and their employ-ees new power plants, water treatment facilities, and transportation and commer-cial construction were required. Meanwhile, Ohio State University began its prodigious expansion in the late 1950s and 1960s. All this growth kept construc-tion workers busy beginning in the 1950s.

Residential construction also exploded during the two decades following the war. Columbus residents and newcomers left decaying inner-city neighborhoods in record numbers for the suburbs, where they could buy new homes with huge backyards at low prices owing to cheap land and low taxes. Bexley and Upper Arlington grew rapidly. In places such as Whitehall, Berwick, and Riverlea developers financed subdivisions on a scale never before seen in the Columbus area. Yet this new construction did not readily translate into a demand for plumbers. Mass production methods, augmented by new plastic pipe technology, contributed to the rise of unskilled, nonunion plumbers. Existing union plumbers found jobs building industrial and commercial structures, but within the union pipefitters soon outnumbered plumbers, whose employment opportunities stagnated.

Pipefitters began to be engaged in new and challenging work. With the addition of air conditioning installation to the work previously done by Local 189 members, mechanical contracting firms became known as heating, ventilating, and air conditioning (HVAC) contractors. Systems to be installed, such as refrigeration, became more complex, requiring specialized skills such as control work, which came into its own in the 1960s. Welding as a way of joining steel pipe quickly displaced cutting and threading in the 1950s. Welding saved time, lasted longer, and was easier to repair. Soon every young journeyman wanted to be a welder.

Many new technological changes originated in the contractors' desire to reduce their wage bill, which had been driven up by the labor shortage. Plumbers began to use copper pipe instead of steel pipe because it was easier to cut, bend, and join, thus saving in wages. Before welding became general, contractors introduced a threading machine that reduced the necessity for much of the labor time and skill of the journeyman. A portable welding machine and portable hacksaw called the "portaband" also came into general use in the 1950s. Contractors introduced smaller and more efficient chainfalls. Electric drills for putting in hangers decreased the cost of installing pipe.

Perhaps the change with the greatest impact on the craft was the widespread adoption of plastic (polyvinyl chloride or PVC) pipe for residential construction purposes. Joining plastic pipe required only a hacksaw, a can of glue, and a minimum of skill. The impact of plastic pipe can be exaggerated, for a good plumber still needed to be familiar with the codes and where and how to run the pipe and vent it. But in nonunion shops these tasks could be performed by a few "lead men" supervising a larger number of lower-paid laborers. The result was a reduction in the demand for skilled plumbers and a great impetus to nonunion forces not only in residential but in light commercial construction as well.

At the same time that deskilling was occurring, some pipefitting work became more intricate and involved. The welds for nuclear power plant piping, for example, had to be checked by x-rays, increasing supervision by the company and decreasing the power of the foreman. Many journeymen began to take seminars in the new technology sponsored by manufacturers. Engineers were hired and became more closely involved in supervising foremen. As the size of the jobs increased, so did the price of finishing behind schedule. To mesh all the diverse tasks undertaken on a construction site efficiently, reducing idle time and maximizing cash flow, contractors in the 1960s adopted the "critical path" approach, which denoted the sequence of tasks and the time each task performed by a journeyman was expected to take. One result of the new drive for efficiency was that "bird-dogging" or "crowding" of journeymen by foremen became more prevalent.

At the same time, it was becoming increasingly difficult for a journeyman to be proficient in all areas of the broadening craft. The overall knowledge and array of skills were simply too great for most journeymen to master. Control work, involving a knowledge of electricity, came into its own as a specialty along with refrigeration and welding. These distinctions within the craft were added to the older one between plumbing and steamfitting.

For all these reasons the coherence of the craft was being threatened as was the ability of journeymen to understand and exercise control over a job. To respond to this challenge and to keep abreast of rapidly changing industrial technology, union leaders, both locally and nationally, realized that they must create a comprehensive and effective apprenticeship program. The goal was nothing less than the creation of a greatly upgraded class of journeymen.

The framework for a national apprenticeship program had been put in place before the war, when the 1937 Fitzgerald Act had authorized the U.S. secretary of labor to set up joint contractor-labor committees to set training standards for each of the building trades. But progress toward apprenticeship was slow. Small employers often found it uneconomical to take their quota of apprentices. Employers who did employ apprentices sometimes laid them off when their term was over and had to pay them full journeyman wages. Also, many journeymen thought employment opportunities were relatively scarce and refused to teach apprentices for fear there would not be enough work to go around.

With the end of the war, a viable apprenticeship training program became a vital necessity recognized by all. A tremendous backlog of civilian construction work faced the industry in the late 1940s, leading to a high demand for skilled craftsmen. The abolition of the helper system in the 1940s left no mechanism other than informal apprenticeship to meet this demand. Further accentuating the need for skilled labor was the relatively high median age of plumbers and pipefitters, which meant that a large number of journeymen would have to be replaced. Finally, strong public support for the aspirations of the large number of returning veterans looking for work meant that government could make tax money available for training purposes.

Between 1946 and 1950 three events converged to create the start of the apprenticeship program in Columbus. Encouraged by the U.S. Department of Labor and the UA along with the Ohio Bureau of Apprenticeship Training, Local 189 set up an apprenticeship committee and called upon contractors to join. On April 29, 1946, the Joint Apprenticeship Committee (JAC) registered with the state of Ohio's Department of Industrial Relations. Meanwhile, the Veterans Administration made available funds for purchasing training materials and paying instructors' salaries. The Columbus school district supplied space.

A loosely knit five-year apprenticeship program was begun in the spring of 1950 with seventy-eight apprentices enrolled in four evening classes in plumbing, steamfitting, and—a new feature—welding. Applicants were accepted either by the union's examining board or by a contractor. Once accepted, they were indentured to their employer, a practice that lasted only until 1950, when the JAC took over the indentures. The JAC set wages, which it raised every six months. Except for war veterans, the program was open only to those seventeen to twenty-five years of age. The union provided instructors for evening classes— most were retired members—and the Columbus School Board paid them. William Beckel, a hardheaded plumber and former naval petty officer from Local 189, put the program together and served as the first apprenticeship coordinator. He worked part time and put in many unpaid hours. Beckel's strong commitment to apprenticeship stemmed from his view that it was a way of paying back servicemen for their wartime sacrifices.

Dick Patterson, apprenticeship coordinator since 1968, remembers what it was like in the 1950s to be an apprentice:

I had an uncle in the local and got in that way. In those days the employer owned us and they even used that term. Once I said that if I don't get a raise I'm going to quit, and they told me you can't do that because "we own you." I went to Central High School two nights a week. We got paid to go to school then. The books that we were using were put out by engineers and were strictly theory, not real training materials. They didn't do us a lot of good. Our welding class had one cutting outfit, two or three welding machines, and fifteen people. We didn't get a hell of a lot of work done. I learned how to play poker because if you couldn't get a welding machine you had to just sit around. The instructors knew their business, but they had no background in instructing and they were older men who had no rapport with the apprentices. But we were in school and I guess it was better than nothing. I wasn't impressed with the school back then, but we did learn to share information and that we were all in the same boat.

The first major improvement in apprenticeship training came in 1957, when the Mechanical Contractors Association of Central Ohio (MCACO) was formed and became affiliated with the Mechanical Contractors of America. Three years later, the union and MCACO established a trust fund collected on the basis of hours worked by journeymen that was earmarked specifically for training purposes. Another turning point in apprenticeship training came in the mid-1960s. But before those changes can be examined, it is necessary to turn to developments in collective bargaining in the 1950s.

Collective Bargaining, 1948–1966

The immediate postwar period was a turbulent time in American labor relations. The ending of wartime price controls unleashed a spiral of inflation, which in turn sparked a massive wave of strikes led by the industrial unions of the CIO. A strike at Timken Roller Bearing in Columbus won by industrial workers with the help of a neutral police force was a major turning point in opening the city to unionism. Soon, however, unions faced a tremendous backlash.

On the national level corporate leaders and conservatives responded to union growth with attempts to revamp the New Deal legal framework that had contributed so much to the rise of unions in the 1930s and 1940s. In 1947 Congress passed the Taft-Hartley Act over President Harry S. Truman's veto. This act, intended to blunt the pro-union thrust of the 1935 Wagner Act, affected the building trades unions by outlawing the closed shop, jurisdictional and secondary boycotts (of nonunion-made materials), and sympathy strikes. All of organized labor strongly opposed Taft-Hartley, and the UA, including Local 189, began funding political action committees to defeat antilabor candidates in 1948 and elect prolabor candidates. When Harry Truman won the presidency in 1948, Local 189 members were elated. They showed their pleasure by making Truman an honorary member of the United Association "for carrying the torch for Organized Labor and the Common Man." The experiences of these years did much to cement the ties between labor and the Democratic party on the national level that had begun during the New Deal.

Labor's continuing power made the application of Taft-Hartley's provisions less

Dick Patterson instructs apprentices.

onerous than at first feared. The closed shop remained in practice, and the courts ruled that nonunion materials could be boycotted through a collective bargaining agreement or when members boycotted of their own volition. The formation of the National Joint Board for the Settlement of Jurisdictional Disputes in 1948 helped quiet the jurisdictional issue. In general, contractors were usually inclined not to antagonize construction unions by using Taft-Hartley, especially during a time of relatively full employment such as existed between 1948 and 1973. In Columbus the contractors took a hands-off attitude toward jurisdictional "wobbles," which continued and even increased during these years. But Taft-Hartley would remain a potent antilabor weapon, available for use by nonunion employers with great effect in the 1970s and 1980s.

Local 189 did not strike during the late 1940s, but it did significantly improve its pay scale and benefit structure. By 1949 Local 189 members were receiving $2.375 an hour, about 50 percent more than the $1.58 they received at the end of the war (during the war they received only an 8 cents-an-hour increase). It responded to the labor shortage and strengthened itself in the industry by taking in helpers as journeymen, organizing large numbers of refrigeration mechanics, and accepting the applications of apprentice plumbers and pipefitters under the new apprenticeship training program. In 1948 alone sixty-five candidates were elected to membership in the local.

Still, the union did not take all candidates into full membership. Gene Brewer, notwithstanding six years of experience in the trade, was one of many dozens of men who were refused entrance into the union and allowed to work only on a temporary permit. Brewer, later a business manager, joined the union after working for two years as a "white-ticket man."

Beginning in 1948 a new set of issues, many of which would later be known as "fringes," joined the perennial concern about wages. One important issue was the provision of double time pay for overtime that had been lost during the war. Travel pay was another topic of contention. In 1937 the jurisdictional area covered by the union had expanded to include the area covered by the Marion, Ohio, local. In 1938 and 1941 Lancaster and Circleville were added and in 1956, Logan, Ohio. Thus, even before 1969, when Chillicothe was added, and 1974, when Newark was added, Local 189 was serving not only Franklin County but greater central Ohio. In the construction boom of the late 1940s many members were working in industrial construction far from their homes in Franklin County, and travel pay was an important issue. In 1948 the local asked the contractors for ten cents per mile for use of their automobiles in the city and five cents per mile out of town, plus single time pay for travel time.

The contractors resisted travel pay mightily because there were so many jobs out of town. The union, however, reiterated the demand each time a contract was negotiated until it was accepted in 1953. The sum awarded per mile increased steadily thereafter as employers began to see it as an incentive to get Franklin County journeymen to travel long distances. Contractors conceded the demand for double time for overtime in 1953, but only for new work. They refused to apply double time to repair work for fear it would price them out of the service work market.

The array of issues known as fringes first became important in the 1950s. To the old-time plumber or fitter, security was not very important. They were used to taking their chances with the vagaries of the labor market. Regarding pensions and health insurance, they tended to prefer the money in take-home pay—"right on the hip" was the saying—and they would take care of their own future. By the early 1950s a slightly younger group of leaders began to take over from the aging patriarchs who had come of age before the war. Hugh H. O'Neill, who had been

Gene Brewer, business manager from 1975 to 1977.

recording secretary for the union as early as 1904–5, again between 1915 and 1920, and then continuously after 1948, finally retired in 1953. O'Neill was a curmudgeon, known to all as a pussycat underneath. Dan Work took over O'Neill's post. The tall, husky Ray Middendorf, who had been financial secretary since 1941, retired in 1951, replaced by Joseph J. Sins. Ed James, business agent since 1943, left the post to Dick Liddil in 1955.

William Beckel, apprenticeship coordinator and president from 1940 to 1942, 1945 to 1953, and 1956 to 1959, provided continuity. Beckel, who worked as superintendent for Roberts Plumbing, was a colorful character, a boisterous, hardheaded "Dutchman" who went strictly "by the book." There was a rule for everything, he thought, and if there wasn't, there ought to be. No man in the history of the union served so many years as president.

The new leaders who came in during the mid-1950s had a somewhat broader, more forward-looking approach. They were less tied to tradition and more open to current trends in the labor movement. In 1947 the United Mine Workers of America won sweeping medical and insurance benefits after a militant strike. In 1949 and 1950 the United Steelworkers and the United Autoworkers won similar fringe packages. This approach contrasted to the traditional practice in the building trades unions of relying on benefits derived from high initiation fees and union dues. It was also different from the approach of other industrialized countries, where government social programs rather than funds derived from collective bargaining provided needed benefits. But by the prosperous 1950s, when the immediate living needs of journeymen were more than fulfilled by pay increases averaging between ten and fifteen cents per year, the idea of insurance funded by contributions from both employers and employees seemed logical to Local 189 members.

The first form of insurance in this period was a revival of the death benefit the local had provided in its early years. In 1948 the local decided that members who wanted to participate in the scheme be assessed $1 at the death of a member, $300 to go to the beneficiary. Later, the fee would be $.50 for each death and $1 for every eighth death. In 1974 the union made the death fund compulsory and added an entry fee to increase its effectiveness (the union now pays a death benefit of $1,200).

In 1949, preparatory to contract negotiations, the union tried to "include some hospitalization fund in our next agreement." This concept was the first break with the past, but it was not taken seriously until the next decade. The following year the local went back to the union-centered approach by establishing a welfare fund for sick and disabled members collected through a $1 assessment on each member. The fund remained in effect for nine years. In 1949, the union asked the contractors for 3 cents in wages as a vacation fund but ended up abandoning the demand in return for a 7.5 cent wage increase.

In 1955, Local 189 took a major step toward a new kind of unionism. Refusing to knuckle under to the contractors, the union declined even to vote on their final offer of a 7.5 cent increase. Plumbers and pipefitters went out on strike for a 22.5 cent increase, with 15 cents to go for a welfare fund, paid holidays, and travel time. After a week on strike, however, the union retreated and accepted a 15 cent wage increase. The old view that health and welfare were less important than take-home pay died hard.

After two more years in which it dropped welfare demands at the last minute in favor of wage increases, the local held out for a welfare increase in 1958. The union took home a 30 cent increase over two years, with 5 cents of it to go toward the establishment of a welfare insurance fund. On July 1, 1958, the local elected its first welfare trustees to take responsibility for the premiums paid to Nationwide Insurance Company. In 1976–77 the union replaced Nationwide with a self-funded plan.

During the first seven years of the 1960s the local completed the basic outlines of its benefit package. In 1962 the union finally won a vacation plan through which 10 cents of the hourly wage would be deposited in Ohio National Bank. Journeymen would be allowed to take out their share once a year, later changed to twice a year. Some used the money for vacations, but most used it for Christmas presents or to live on during times of unemployment. A group of younger members, including Brewer, Ed Scanlon, Roy Taylor, and John Bowser, Sr., traveled on their own initiative throughout the state to investigate the pension plans of other locals and, after considerable resistance, prevailed on the union leadership to sponsor a pension plan. In 1965 the union decided to start its first pension—though it would not be fully established until two years later—by voting eighty-two to thirty-five to apply 15 cents due in June 1966 to an old age insurance fund. During all this time the prosperity in the industry continued, allowing for an increase in pay from $3.45 in December 1957 to $4.645 in 1966.

As membership grew from less than 400 at the end of the war in 1945 to 765 in 1960 and its wealth increased, the internal life of Local 189 became much more diverse and elaborate. Though dues had increased at a rate only about half that of pay since the war, the union in 1967 funded softball, basketball, tag football, and bowling teams in addition to the annual picnic. These activities replaced the old-time stag affairs that often ended in fistfights—one Columbus police officer is said to have remarked that he would not have taken $500 to work at a plumbers' and fitters' picnic. The list of committees an active member could belong to included labor-management, pension, joint apprenticeship, organizing, political education and legislative, welfare, hospital insurance, entertainment and picnic, and softball. The union could also afford to pay the full expenses of those attending conventions and daily wages for members serving as election officials. The union gave regularly to organized charities, most notably the United Appeal. In 1964 the local decided to leave its hall at 555 E. Rich Street, where rampant crime had forced it to pay $3 a month for police protection, and purchased a building at 841 Alton Avenue, which was named Richard Anderson Hall after the local's recently deceased president. The local hired its first full-time office secretary in 1966.

To service its expanded geographical jurisdiction and membership, the union in 1961 added Frank Crowley as an assistant business agent to Dick Liddil. One year later the local created the new office of business manager, filled by Liddil. The business manager became the full-time coordinator of the affairs of the local from the office. Crowley moved up to business agent. In 1968 Joseph J. Snyder was hired as a second business agent, and by 1977 there were three men in the position.

The Curley Steiner Era

The last half of the 1960s was a turbulent time in America. With the passage of the 1964 Civil Rights Act, Martin Luther King, Jr.'s civil rights movement gave way to black nationalism and urban ghetto riots born of years of racism and frustration. The intensification of the Vietnam War inspired tens of thousands of students to take to the streets in antiwar demonstrations culminating in the incredible scenes at the Democratic National Convention in 1968. Meanwhile, hippies tried to inaugurate a countercultural alternative to America's conformist, materialistic society. Few Local 189 members identified with these movements. In fact, the UA formally endorsed the Vietnam War effort. In 1970 the local built a flagpole and flew an American flag to demonstrate publicly its patriotic support of the government.

Yet it is ironic that the most militant and successful period in the union's history coincided almost precisely with the heyday of militant students and blacks. The common denominator underpinning both upsurges was the prosperous, full-employment economy of the 1960s that evoked hopes and expectations of racial, social, and economic equality on the part of young Americans who, in varying degrees, felt left out of the American dream.

The man who symbolized the new spirit within the union and who led it into a new era was Dudley "Curley" Steiner. Steiner was a colorful, impulsive, generous, charismatic figure who represented the ascendance of a younger generation that had come of age during World War II and afterward. Born in Texas, Steiner had been a paratrooper in the right flank of General George Patton's army in Europe and had been dropped into the German-surrounded city of Bastogne during the German counterattack in the Battle of the Bulge. After joining the union, Steiner soon made a name for himself at meetings as an aggressive union man. When one member at a meeting in 1956 proposed that Westinghouse strikers be given $100, Steiner jumped up and proposed raising the figure to $1,000. In 1962 his protest of his loss in the election for business manager led to the appointment of a committee to write up a set of local by-laws that could be published and disseminated.

Steiner soon became the spokesman for the younger members, who had swelled the ranks of the union during the 1950s and early 1960s and thought the older leadership was not making enough progress in contracts, and was freezing them out of jobs. Steiner often complained that a person could not speak at meetings unless "you had gray in your hair." He was dissatisfied especially with Dick Liddil's regime as business agent and business manager. Liddil was an intelligent man, but he was soft-spoken and conciliatory, the very opposite of Steiner. Beginning in 1962, when Steiner challenged Liddil in the first election for business manager, a faction polarized around each man. The core of the Liddil group was the older members and the "steady Eddies," while the younger fitters and plumbers who had less job security coalesced around Steiner. Steiner lost, but in 1964 he ran again on the issue of ending hiring by contractors outside of the hiring hall—appealing directly to those who couldn't get steady work—and on this basis defeated Liddil.

That same year work had begun on the Anheuser-Busch Brewery, a project that would provide jobs for three years. Construction of the brewery in Worthington had an enormous impact on the union—both positive and negative. At one time approximately three hundred of the union's five hundred active members were employed on that job. Ten-hour days, six days a week—"six-tens" in fitter or plumber parlance—were common, and overtime was paid at double time. The work was slow-paced. One major impact of the brewery job was that men who were working in residential plumbing, in light commercial, and even at a water treatment plant left those fields for the assured overtime and job security of the brewery. This undercut the ability of union contractors to maintain their niche in less attractive fields and resulted in their abandonment to nonunion contractors.

But the immediate impact of the brewery was the leverage it gave the union over local contractors. For years the union had settled for substantially less than it had asked for during bargaining. The men who had elected Steiner grumbled that pay was substantially less than in comparable cities and that recent increases were being eaten up by "creeping inflation." They saw this job as the chance to "jam it to the contractors."

But the union members had more than Steiner to encourage their militance. In 1966 Gene Evans, known as a "radical union man" and of the same generation as Steiner, had been elected president. Before contract negotiations, Evans received permission from the local to serve on the negotiating committee. More important, he received full authority to suspend union meetings during the expected strike until the committee had a contract it deemed adequate to submit to the membership. By abandoning the traditional practice of holding meetings during a strike, Evans hoped to circumvent the contractors' influence on the union through their steady men. It was an approach that set an important precedent for future union practice.

When the strike started in June 1967, hundreds of journeymen got jobs out of town, and the rest found work at the brewery. The general contractor at Busch, H. K. Ferguson, who was not a member of the MCACO but rather a signatory to the national agreement, hired the strikers over the heads of the local contractors who were being struck. Ernie Ware, who came in to head the Mechanical Contractors Association soon after the strike, remembers: "Instead of being on strike, members of local 189 were actually all working at the brewery. Union men were sitting there with a smile on their faces: 'Gee we're not hurting, we're all working.' What else could the contractor do but give them what they asked for?"

When the two-month strike ended on August 1, the union had won a tremendous victory. In its three-year contract, Local 189 won pay increases of $.81 the first year, $1.20 the second year, and $1.12 the third year. Over three years the increase translated into a 67 percent wage raise, not including fringe benefits. Moreover, it set a precedent that allowed the union to win one dollar raises for each of the next three years of the 1970–73 contract. At one point in the contract period, Columbus plumbers and pipefitters surpassed those of San Francisco and New York, having the highest wage in the nation within the trade.

But wages were only part of the victory. The union won a jointly administered pension plan funded by a 15-cent-per-hour employer contribution the first year and 20 cents in 1969. The plan allowed members to retire at age sixty-five if they had ten years of continuous union membership. Employers' contributions were based on at least eighteen hundred hours—about two years—of steady work. Members who wanted to retire at age fifty-five could do so though the pension was smaller.

The 1967 strike was a turning point in the union's history. The negotiating committee consisted of the following members: (seated, from left to right) Curley Steiner, Gene Evans, and Vince McCarthy; (standing, from left to right) Denny Reynolds, Bill Dolph, Frank Kelley, and Charles Moore.

In the same contract the union won greatly increased funding of the apprenticeship training program, which benefited both journeymen and union contractors. The employer now paid apprentices directly to attend day rather than evening school, a feature that established a powerful incentive for apprentices to study harder and opened up evening classes for retraining journeymen. The apprenticeship program also significantly upgraded its training. Refrigeration and air conditioning training, which had been introduced during the early 1960s supported by a UA-NCA (National Contractors Association) fund, was improved, and the training school, located since 1964 at 841 Alton Avenue, bought the equipment to teach TIG welding (often called "heli-arc") that was used at the brewery. Since this period Local 189 and the MCACO have been able to boast of having one of the finest UA apprenticeship training programs in the United States.

Important improvements were also made in hiring hall procedures, Steiner's major campaign issue. In 1959 the union had set up a formal hiring hall system to comply with a court decision based on the Taft-Hartley Act. In 1964 the union had increased the fine for circumventing the out-of-work list from $5 to $100. Still, there was no numerical list in the hall, and even those who did use the hall were subject to discriminatory practices favoring members who had established themselves with contractors or the business agents. The present financial secretary-treasurer, Charles Gronbach, remembers as a young journeyman waiting in the hall for work, while an older member came in and went right back out with a job.

The 1967 agreement greatly strengthened the hiring hall by putting the obligation to be fair on the employer. According to article 16 of the contract: "Whenever new or additional Employees are needed, the Employer shall notify the Union in writing, stating the location, starting time, approximate duration of the job, type of work to be performed and number of workmen requested." Further to enforce use of the hiring hall, those referred to jobs were given "introduction slips," which the employer had to return by mail within twenty-four hours. When they were finished with a job, journeymen were to be given "termination slips" that qualified them to be placed on the out-of-work list.

Though employers and journeymen often circumvented hiring hall procedures, the 1967 agreement established the modern hiring hall and brought major advances for the union in establishing enforceable rules in hiring, thereby strengthening the union by minimizing the dependence of journeymen on the good graces of particular contractors.

Yet in one glaring area the 1967 contract introduced an element of unfairness and discord in hiring hall procedure that would open a deep wound within the union's membership and undermine Steiner's leadership. The agreement divided those employed by contractors into three "seniority" groups: Group 1 included men who had been employed at least twelve hundred hours per year for five consecutive years; Group 2 consisted of the rest of the union's members, approximately 10 to 15 percent, mostly younger men; Group 3 was made up of nonunion workmen with at least one year's experience who could be hired by contractors on a temporary basis subject to union work rules, union scale, and payment of union dues. Men in this latter category were known as "permit men" or "white-ticket men" and were to be hired only when union journeymen were not available (largely because so many were working on the brewery or out of town).

According to the contract, no Group 2 men could be taken out of the hiring hall until all Group 1 men had been hired; conversely, no Group 1 men could be laid off until all Group 2 men had been laid off. What started as a well-intentioned effort to adopt some form of union-guaranteed seniority and job security, similar to typical union agreements in mass production industries, created bitter enmity within the union. When employment opportunities declined in 1968, Group 2 men soon found themselves unable to find any work out of the hall and had to go on the road. Even a UA journeyman of long standing, the business agent of Chillicothe Local 723 with forty-eight years of service, who had come into 189 when his local merged with it in 1969, was denied Group 1 status. Group 2 members felt stigmatized. Pat Ferry, later president of the local and at that time in Group 2, was once rebuked by a Group 1 man with the words, "You're not as good a mechanic." Group 2 member Jim Weaver said the seniority clause made him feel like "half a member." Many younger men had bitter feelings toward Evans and others who had negotiated the contract and toward Steiner, who as business manager had to enforce it.

The Entrance of Blacks and Women

Before the Civil Rights Act of 1964 took effect in the construction industry, Local 189, like most other UA locals, was a loosely knit clique limited to relatives of those already in the union. This "club atmosphere" furthered the transmission of skills and customs from generation to generation, but it excluded all outsiders, men and women, white and black, who were potentially qualified and might want to work at the trade.

There is no doubt that the union as a whole shared the racial attitudes of most white Americans and until the 1960s operated with an unofficial "color bar." So shameless was racial discrimination that Francis Wolfe remembers one local president in the 1960s declaring, "There will never be a nigger in this local." When the civil rights movement accelerated in the 1960s, it was not uncommon for white journeymen to assert that they would refuse to work beside a black journeyman. In 1968 the openly racist candidate for U.S. president, George Wallace, had a small but vocal following in Local 189.

The first break in this pattern came in 1967, during a time of labor shortage when the contractors decided to hire white-ticket men as stipulated in the contract. A union committee passed over a black permit member named Gwylard Locke in favor of a white member. In 1967 the state Equal Employment Opportunity Commission (EEOC) filed a suit against Local 189 on behalf of Locke in U.S. District Court on the basis of Title VII of the 1964 Civil Rights Act. On May 29, 1968, the judge found in favor of the plaintiff. He awarded Locke $10,000 and ordered the union to renegotiate articles 15 and 16 of its 1967 agreement concerning hiring hall procedures. In 1968 the articles were renegotiated and approved by the court. Meanwhile, the union let in its first two black journeymen along with sixty-six other applicants in an attempt to avoid an affirmative action court decree.

In May 1969 the EEOC petitioned that the renegotiated articles, though guaranteeing nondiscrimination, did not attempt to correct the effects of years of past discrimination. The decision of the court again went against the union, and during the next three years the local spent over $10,000 fighting it in courts of appeal. The attitude of Local 189 mirrored that of the UA nationally, which fought affirmative action vigorously before acquiescing to its inevitability in 1968.

In October 1972 the union accepted a consent decree handed down by Judge Joseph P. Kinneary that stipulated the following key provisions, creating what has been called "superseniority": (1) all black journeymen were to be considered part of Group 1; (2) applicants for membership were not required to have experience in union shops but could count experience in nonunion shops or the armed forces; (3) black members were not required to pass any examination to be part of the hiring hall system except one that met EEOC guidelines, and this provision applied only to members who had not worked before 1968; (4) Local 189 was to establish a special affirmative action register for licensed black journeymen with five years' experience in the trade to allow them to bump white journeymen for purposes of fulfilling affirmative action goals set by the EEOC; (5) black applicants were to pay the initiation fee of $72, not the increased fee of $850 established after the strike, and they could take three years to pay the fee in installments. The court order was to remain in effect for five years.

With the 1973 contract about to be negotiated, the 1972 consent decree consolidated an emerging consensus in the union against the seniority rules regarding groups 1 and 2. Responding to sentiment from the local's membership for greater fairness as well as pressure for affirmative action from the court, the union's negotiators decided to scrap the 1967–72 hiring hall procedure and negotiate a hall with ironclad rules designed to guarantee fairness. According to the 1973–76 agreement, job applicants would be divided into two groups based on residence or nonresidence in the jurisdictional area; within each group the out-of-work list was to be kept in strict chronological order of the dates the men qualified for employment. To guarantee fairness, the contract set up a labor-management appeals committee, including one "public" member, to consider employment complaints. When layoffs occurred, residents were to have priority over nonresidents, but there was to be no seniority within each group. For the first time, the contract required contractors employing more than six journeymen to hire one journeyman, fifty-five years or older, for every six journeymen they hired from the hall.

Meanwhile, the union's apprenticeship program had begun to feel the full effect of affirmative action. In 1969 a representative from the Limbach Company, while touting the apprenticeship program at Columbus high schools, had mistakenly announced that anyone passing an aptitude test—prepared by Ohio State University professor Wilbur Stover for the union in 1966—would be hired automatically. He failed to mention that applicants would be placed on a list ranked by test scores. When a black teenager passed the test and was not accepted into the program because he was low on the list, he filed suit with the EEOC against the Limbach Company. The JAC took over the case but lost after being unable to demonstrate to the court that its test was applicable to the industry. After spending approximately $15,000 in court fees, the JAC accepted a ten-year consent decree from U.S. District Court judge Karl B. Rubin in July 1972. It required the JAC to take in blacks as its first ten apprentices and accept 11 to 12 percent blacks in future entering classes. The ten new apprentices joined two other black apprentices who had entered the program in 1968. The decree also ended the written test and substituted oral interviews. Since accepting the consent decree, the JAC also attempts to conform to the affirmative action standards set by the U.S. Department of Labor's Bureau of Apprenticeship Training.

Besides opening its program to blacks, the revamping of JAC practices provided an unexpected boon to the union in helping contractors who wanted to bid for state work to meet affirmative action goals set by the EEOC. Many black journeymen might not want to work for a contractor who needed a certain number of blacks to meet his affirmative action goal, but the JAC could assign a black apprentice to the job, thus meeting the EEOC requirement.

In many instances the entrance of blacks into the union had a positive effect on white journeymen's racial attitudes. Most whites accepted black journeymen on the job as equals and as union brothers as long as they demonstrated skill as competent and reliable mechanics. Affirmative action, however, had and continues to have few defenders among white journeymen because of the widespread perception that less than competent black journeymen were kept on the job simply to fill quotas. This fueled a generalized resentment, even though the 1972 consent decree lapsed in 1977, because whites were often asked by business agents to allow blacks lower on the hiring hall list to jump ahead of them to let contractors meet their affirmative action requirements. The number of blacks increased slowly. In 1989 there were forty-four black members of Local 189, about 4.5 percent of active members.

The prospect of women entering the trade was hardly even contemplated by union journeymen until the late 1970s. Opposition to women entering the trade was probably even greater than toward blacks. Women were not considered physically strong enough to perform heavy lifting tasks, nor were their sensibilities considered suited to the graphic sexual language so prevalent on the job. Some journeymen's wives worried about possible on-the-job romances taking away their husbands. The unofficial saying was that women's place "was in the home, not the crawl space."

In the 1970s contractors had met federal and state pressure on contractors to bring women into the trade by pointing to the women they had hired as clerks or truck drivers. In 1979 the JAC began to accept women into the apprenticeship program. The character of the first crop of female apprentices, including Cindy Coffland, Vici Gleich, Teri Warren (later Warren Dominguez), Kathy Howard Ely, and Karen Frank, did not conform to the prejudices of male journeymen. They were not the dainty and demure maidens of stereotype. Surprising some journeymen, they performed their tasks competently and were able to handle the razzing that they—along with male apprentices—received from older journeymen. They also parried the inevitable come-ons, all without resorting to calling on business agents for help. The fact that most of these women came from families of construction workers helped in the transition.

This is not to say that women did not confront deep-seated difficulties in the trade or in the union. Some among the later groups of female apprentices did not have the strength or the stamina for the work and dropped out. Others got married and had babies and either left the trade or became part-time workers. A severe and enduring obstacle for women has been the male construction job culture marked by continual testing of one another, verbal sexual sparring and joking, and often outright harassment of women. To be part of it was to lose one's sense of femininity; yet to be outside of it was to become isolated and a victim.

Another obstacle, just as significant, was and is that married women are expected to handle the draining physical and emotional burden of homemaking and child rearing *in addition* to putting in a full eight hours plus occasional overtime on a physically demanding job. Moreover, their husbands or boyfriends are often jealous of their spending time at work or at union meetings with eligible men. The demands of being a "superwoman" are greatest on married women plumbers and fitters, but a few like Teri Warren Dominguez have adapted well.

Women have not had a great impact on the male members of the local. In 1989 there were fourteen women members of the union, about 1.5 percent of the active members. One positive development is that when some vocal women asked for drinking water and clean toilets on jobs, male journeymen supported them and stopped accepting excuses on the part of some contractors.

The Close of the Steiner Era

Curley Steiner's influence in the union reached its peak in the late 1960s. He was immensely popular with the members. Not only before his campaign for office but afterward as well, Steiner often would spend the evening into the morning hours drinking with his large circle of admirers and friends, each of whom he would address affectionately as "hoss" and upon whom he might spend his entire paycheck. Rank-and-file members could talk honestly and intimately with him and get straight answers, and he would go to bat for those he felt had legitimate grievances and back them to the hilt. To Steiner there were two sides, labor and management, and little in between. He constantly tested the limits of collective bargaining. During negotiations, he would often cuss and stamp his feet, which irritated the contractors. But Steiner was knowledgeable in labor law and union matters. He would shoot down crack-brained schemes offered at union meetings. He was respected by other business agents throughout the state and was instrumental in uniting different UA locals in Ohio for common ends such as reciprocity agreements. Steiner, by his charismatic example, introduced a new standard for leadership in Local 189.

But Steiner had weak points that would eventually lead to his downfall. He was a diabetic, and his inability to control his drinking had serious effects on his health and on his effectiveness as a leader. Even a few beers might put him to sleep during the day. In 1967 he easily defeated the attempt of Gene Evans to unseat him. But after almost a decade of service his drinking took its toll. In December

*Dudley "Curley" Steiner speaking at the seventy-fifth anniversary
celebration of Local 189 in 1975.*

1973 this issue plus the Group 1–Group 2 dispute led a majority of Local 189 members to cast their votes for Gene Brewer for business manager. In his farewell statement Steiner delivered a humorous, upbeat address. "Hoss," he told the members, "you ain't seen the last of me yet. I'll be back or there ain't a cow in Texas."

And he was right. The next year he ran for business agent but was defeated in a close vote. Not a man to accept defeat easily, Steiner protested the election to the UA because a contractor had sent out a letter to Local 189 members favoring his opponent, Charlie Smithers. The UA overturned the election and Steiner was elected in a new vote, serving until 1982. But the Curley Steiner era had come to a close. In his last years Steiner lost both his legs to diabetes and his drinking habit, and he hobbled around the office on artificial legs. But till his death in 1985 he never lost his sense of humor or gave way to self-pity.

During the years from World War II to 1973, highlighted by Steiner's leadership, the union underwent the most important transformation in its history. Membership in the local more than doubled in less than twenty years. Skill and pride in workmanship, so strong among plumbers and fitters, found an outlet in the creation, together with the MCACO, of one of the finest apprenticeship training programs in the country. Perhaps the most important institutional accomplishments in this period were the strictly enforced rules in the hiring hall guaranteeing fairness and the independence of the union from the influence of contractors. It is one of the ironies of the union's history that the modern hiring hall, which benefits all members, grew in part from the affirmative action court decree that the union resisted so strenuously.

The influence of Curley Steiner would live on through his protégés, the young journeymen with whom he drank and whom he educated in new ways of leadership, who came into office in the mid- to late 1970s: men such as Danie Lewis, John Noll, Bill McAfee, Charlie Gronbach, Gene Minix, Bob Dyer, and Dick Patterson. But the union was about to face its most formidable challenge: how to organize the growing number of nonunion workers in its jurisdiction and how far to go in assisting union contractors in meeting the growing competition from nonunion contractors.

5. A Fight for Survival: The Nonunion Challenge, 1970–1989

By the late 1960s Local 189 had achieved an unprecedented level of prosperity for its members. In pay scale and benefits it had risen to national leadership; its apprentice training program was second to none; and its hiring hall was the envy of other construction locals. Local 189 could boast an aggressive, forward-looking leadership. And yet, while all these things were being accomplished, storm clouds were gathering on the horizon.

Light residential work had always been the domain of small-scale, nonunion contractors, but in the past few of them had ventured out of this preserve. Large apartment projects, as well as commercial and industrial construction, were reserved for union contractors employing union journeymen. As late as 1958 about a third of Local 189's membership—all plumbers—worked on large housing projects on the expanding east side of the city. They were employed by small-scale union plumbing and heating contracting firms such as Zack, Roberts, Rinehardt, and Carlisle.

The unprecedented industrial, commercial, and residential expansion of Columbus in the 1950s, accelerating in the 1960s, undermined this traditional demarcation of work. MCACO contractors concentrated their efforts on large, lucrative industrial and commercial jobs in the city center and in the suburbs. Local 189 members followed, attracted by the stable employment and plentiful overtime offered by these jobs. Gradually, union contractors withdrew from competitive bidding, first the larger residential and then the smaller commercial jobs. Slowly but inevitably, this shift created a vacuum at the lower end of the employment spectrum that was filled by nonunion contractors employing nonunion men.

Like a metastasizing cancer, the nonunion sector expanded during the 1960s, by default taking over the competitively bid jobs abandoned by union contractors and union journeymen. It came to a head in the late 1960s, when the best union journeymen flocked to the brewery to work 6-10s (a six-day, 10-hour-a-day week) and 7-10s at the high wages won by the 1967 strike, disdaining the small, one-month jobs, the dirty jobs in the ditch, and the less-skilled jobs. A high $850 initiation fee tended to keep out new journeymen while high wages won in 1967 helped price the union's plumbers out of the residential work. The nonunion sector accelerated its growth in those years, and then, and only then, did the union wake up. But it was too late. Once nonunion contractors had proven their competence to builders, they established a foothold that was difficult to dislodge. The trend continued through the 1970s and 1980s, bringing underemployment to the local's members and making a mockery of the high wages and high benefits that the local had achieved, except for those favored with full-time employment.

None of this was inevitable. Almost all the skilled craftsmen in the region were within the union's ranks in the mid-1960s, and they possessed inherent advantages in competition with lower-paid nonunion journeymen. Few nonunion contractors were militantly antiunion, and under different circumstances the local might have organized much of the nonunion sector. Yet this did not happen. Why it did not and what the union has tried to do to make up for lost time is the subject of this chapter.

The Good Times End

In 1958 two young nonunion journeymen went to the union hall to apply to the union's examining board for membership in Local 189. They were told they had to take a proficiency test and were given a date to come back. Four times they showed up, and each time they were told to come back again. One journeyman came back a fifth time. He took and passed the test and joined the union. The other gave up and decided to take his master's test from the city and go into business for himself in January 1959 as a nonunion contractor. Throughout most of the 1960s the contractor confined his business to the residential field, but by the late 1960s he had expanded into light commercial work and by the 1970s he was into the more lucrative end of the commercial market. In 1980, Local 189 business agent Danie Lewis wrote that the contractor, Jim Croson, is "the biggest nonunion thorn in our side," with "several million dollars worth of work going on in our jurisdiction."

The story of Jim Croson illustrates graphically and painfully the nature of the problem facing the union. For any craft union, such as the plumbers and pipefitters, to be successful, it must take into membership all those journeymen skilled enough to retain employment in the trade. When employers in the late nineteenth and early twentieth centuries recognized the success of the union in achieving this goal, they had no choice but to sign collective bargaining agreements to gain access to that pool of skilled labor in their geographical area. Collective bargaining, in turn, contributed to the stability of the entire industry. Yet once they had become members of the union, skilled journeymen had a short-term interest in limiting the number of new members entering the union so as to maximize employment opportunities for themselves. There was and remains a strong tendency for all craft unions, including Local 189, to become ingrown "clubs" employing various tests to exclude otherwise qualified journeymen, while allowing employers to increase their work forces only through temporary "permit men." Once this occurs, the union no longer has a lock on the pool of skilled journeymen.

Thus there are two imperatives working at loggerheads within a craft union: the inclusionist and exclusionist. When the exclusionist tendency predominates, it is only a matter of time before the number of excluded but competent journeymen increases to the point that the nonunion sector can challenge the union sector in all areas of the trade. Jim Croson was only one of a growing number of journeymen who were allowed "to slip through the net" during the postwar period. For the union, the consequences were chilling.

With the slowdown of the incredible building spree of the 1960s in 1968 and the recession and rising unemployment of 1969, Local 189 became aware of the pressing need to organize its jurisdiction more thoroughly. In 1969 the organizing committee, which had lain dormant since its founding after the war, was reactivated and began to try to organize the open shops. The organizing method was "top down." The union mailed letters to the open shops explaining to them the advantages of signing a collective bargaining agreement. It didn't work. This failure was the genesis of a long train of contract givebacks by the union that slowed but did not reverse the nonunion tide.

In the fall of 1970, when the nonunion share of the large jobs was approaching 50 percent and approximately one-third of the union's active membership was on the out-of-work list, Curley Steiner, who had come from a nonunion shop himself, decided to approach the MCACO with a proposal that the contractors get back into the lost residential market. The MCACO, representing sixty-one member and forty nonmember companies in a ten-county area, replied that it would do so only if the union would grant concessions. After numerous meetings both sides settled on a $4.36 an hour wage cut from the regular wage (take-home plus fringes) of $10.52 (there was no cut in fringes) to apply to residential structures not exceeding three stories. The new wage was determined by matching the average of the wages paid by some of the better nonunion residential builders. The key feature of the agreement was a stipulation that once a journeyman accepted work under the residential agreement, he could not quit the job until it was completed, even if a higher-paying commercial or industrial job was available. To counteract a possible shortage of manpower, the union agreed that if they could not find union members, after forty-eight hours employers would be free to hire temporary workmen. The union rationalized that these journeymen, drawn from nonunion ranks, could easily be signed up for the union by Local 189's business agents with the approval of MCACO employers.

The agreement, signed in October 1971, was the first of its kind in the industry in the United States. An article detailing its provisions was published in a prominent contractors' journal the following year accompanied by a photograph picturing Curley Steiner standing proudly between MCACO executive director Ernie Ware and MCACO president Sam Shuman. Both sides expressed optimism. "I can see no problems," said Steiner. "If the business warrants it we will establish a [training] school to provide all the men needed. For the present, if we can't provide the people, we'll let the contractor get his own. We are serious about the residential contract, and will do all that is in our power to make this a workable situation." As Ernie Ware put it: "Although our members are not residentially oriented by tradition, and we really haven't gone after this market as much as we might, the day is fast approaching when both these situations are going to turn 180 degrees. The prospects of getting residential work are available and we're going to get our share."

The agreement was approved by the local in a ballot, along with a similar one covering water treatment plants. But the turnaround was only a few degrees, not the 180 Ware predicted. Work picked up and unemployment fell among union members. Few MCACO contractors bid on residential jobs because the profit margin on such small jobs was too low. Nor did they pick up new contractors to do the work.

While all this was going on, the union's meteoric ascent into the higher reaches of the pay scale had run into an immovable object: the federal government. After 1967 a wage-price spiral originating in the Vietnam-era inflation had approached intolerable double-digit levels. In 1971 the Republican administration of Richard Nixon opted for federal wage-price controls overseen in the construction industry by a stabilization committee composed of representatives of labor and capital and chaired by former Department of Labor secretary John Dunlop. According to the three-year 1970 contract, Local 189 members were to receive an increase in gross pay (not counting fringes or deductions) from $9.67 in 1971 to $10.71 in 1972. But this was not to be. The stabilization board disallowed the raise.

The union went back to negotiations with MCACO and in 1973 presented the wage stabilization board with a new package, which was approved. Instead of a wage increase, the men received a fifteen-cent increase in pension contribution and a ten-cent increase for health and welfare. At a special meeting local members decided to divide another thirty-five cents four ways. Two cents went for wages in the paycheck; three cents into the organizing fund. Of the rest, Local 189 sent fifteen cents into the national pension fund, joining the UA program for the first time. With the other fifteen cents the local placated its younger members by establishing a supplemental unemployment benefits (SUB) fund administered by a joint board of trustees. Beginning in April 1976 SUB offered $25 a week for twenty-six weeks, then $50 a week for the next twenty-six weeks (initial SUB funds increased to $45 a week in 1979). SUB acted as a supplement—and in some cases substitute—for state unemployment compensation. Unfortunately, SUB came too late to help during the 1974 recession and went out of existence in 1982.

The new total package was worth $11.12, resulting in a sixty-five-cent-an-hour decrease in the compensation due the men according to the 1970 agreement—a windfall for the contractors. Plumber George Meany, then AFL-CIO president, led the criticism of the way the wage guidelines were being implemented by the Nixon administration. Local 189 members were especially irate because wages were being frozen but not profits. Gross pay remained at the $9.67 level until the 1974 contract increased pay to $10.42 in June of that year, $11.02 in June 1975, and $11.17 in December 1975. In sum, local members, who had received $5.03 in wage increases in the four years between 1967 and 1971, received $1.50 in wage increases during the succeeding four years. These paltry increases, combined with substantial continuing inflation and low employment levels, translated into a lowered standard of living for most members of the local.

Although many members blamed the government, the underlying reason for stagnating or falling living standards was the continuing rise of the nonunion sector. In 1972 the frustration of unionized construction workers with the growth of nonunion contracting in the commercial sector led them to resort to the direct action methods that construction workers in Chicago, New York, and Philadelphia have traditionally relied on during labor conflicts throughout the last century. The spark came when nonunion contractors employed by Charles W. Bonner Company were hired to build the French Market, a huge city within a city complex located at the intersection of Route 161 and Busch Boulevard. Also known as the Continent, it was to include apartments, a hotel, restaurant, theater, tennis courts, and shopping mall. It was the first large commercial job done by nonunion labor in the Columbus area.

On September 13, 1972, three hundred union demonstrators blocked Busch Boulevard; the next day, fifteen hundred hard hats took the day off from work to participate in another demonstration, which they followed up with a march to the statehouse. On October 23, after a month of unproductive negotiations with the Bonner Company, about four hundred frustrated journeymen gathered in front of the French Market site. They wore red armbands to distinguish themselves from nonunion workers. Once assembled, the union workers pulled down or spoiled recently completed work at the project, set fires, and wrecked equipment. The men then split up into trades groups and went to different scab building sites in the city. At Ohio State University, Local 189 members confronted nonunion mechanics working for Jim Croson and drove them off the site. The day of direct action resulted in over six hundred thousand dollars worth of damage at construction sites throughout Columbus.

The *Columbus Dispatch* called the affair a rampage and, in an editorial, the *Citizens-Journal* deplored the violence. Some union contractors protested the damage as well. But the action was consistent with the traditional rough-and-tumble code of ethics that had long governed the behavior of construction workers. American building trades unions originated in a crucible of violent conflict; among many unionized building tradesmen only the effectiveness of the French Market affair, not its morality, was at issue. By that criterion, their direct action had considerable potential. It demonstrated to the entire city that the various unionized building trades workmen were ready to act together as a group, and their willingness to engage in highly risky acts proved their determination to defend their livelihoods. Clearly, they were in earnest; they had drawn a line in the sand and dared the nonunion element to cross it.

If the construction unions had followed up their September 13 action with mass public demonstrations, taking their case directly to the working people of the Columbus metropolitan area, the energy and determination aroused might have worked to the unions' advantage. But within a week of the action, the Building Trades Council and union leaders were hit with a $5.6-million lawsuit. Leaders backed away from the issue, leaving the enthusiasm and anger of the younger members and much of the rank and file to fester in public silence.

The negative consequences of the French Market affair soon became apparent. Many nonunion contractors, frightened by their vulnerability to mass action, joined the militantly antiunion Associated Builders and Contractors (ABC), a nationwide organization of seventeen thousand nonunion contractors that had already established a chapter in Columbus. The ABC offered the nonunion contractors legal counsel, group insurance, tactical advice on how to respond to union organizing drives, and mutual consolation and support. Later, the ABC established training facilities—though inferior to those provided by the JAC—to produce nonunion journeymen. The growth of the ABC in the mid-1970s consolidated the nonunion sector and gave it leadership.

In 1975 construction activity in Columbus suffered a major downturn. The dollar volume based on permit awards fell 40 percent from 1974. The union's out-of-work list swelled by the end of the year to 380 men. As early as January 1975 the idea of instituting a thirty-two-hour workweek had been considered at a special meeting but was rejected because it would have violated the existing contract. On November 8, when the local met to discuss contract proposals for the 1976 agreement, discussion again centered on ways to relieve unemployment. Some of the proposals were as follows: a shorter (thirty-five-hour) workweek; extending the numbers of days a member could hold a job from five days to three weeks during which time he could retain his place on the hiring hall list; rotating jobs among all the members; and removing the ninety-day recall period (the contract allowed employers to "recall" a journeyman within ninety days of layoff even if that journeyman was at the bottom of the list). Ultimately it was decided to demand the removal of the ninety-day recall provision and a pay increase.

In June 1976, with a resurgence in construction activity but mild unemployment persisting, Local 189 and MCACO settled on a moderate four-step increase in gross pay from $11.17 to $12.47 over two years. Employers' contributions to the different fringe funds remained the same as in the previous contract.

A New Strategy

By the mid-1970s a new pattern had been established in union-contractor relations. The union moderated its demands to the MCACO, mainly attempting to preserve the gains of previous years. Simultaneously, it began to reorient its energies to dealing with the growth of the nonunion sector. When direct action failed, the union took a three-pronged approach.

One prong dealt with the unwillingness of the MCACO contractors to bid on the smaller jobs, by default leaving the work to nonunion contractors. The local decided to encourage its journeyman members to go into business for themselves as contractors, thus increasing the number of small contractors who would both bid on the smaller work and use the union's hiring hall. The movement of journeymen into the ranks of contractors was not, of course, new. Such upward mobility had been continuous for over a hundred years. Indeed, the vast majority of contractors were former union journeymen, and many retained their union cards. This enabled them to keep their benefits, and if they failed in business they could always go back to the hiring hall. What was new was the union's active encouragement of the process.

Section 178 of the UA constitution, which prevented members who had become contractors or who owned stock in their employer's business from retaining a voice in the union, was a major obstacle to taking this tactic. This constitutional provision grew out of the union's need to maintain independence from the influence of the contractors. Despite appeal from Local 189 in 1976 the UA refused to change its interpretation of the constitution, but many union contractors continued to retain their union membership and benefits by transferring ownership rights to their wives or relatives, though they could not vote at union meetings.

Jim Ely, president of Local 189 in 1971, became a successful contractor doing automatic control work and employing twelve union journeymen, including two of his sons and one daughter-in-law. When Mead Corporation in Chillicothe was about to hire a nonunion contractor, Local 189's business agent, Bill Steinhauser, helped Allan Hale, a journeyman respected by the company as well as the members of the local, to start a contracting firm to fill that niche and employ union journeymen. During slack periods, Hale does not maximize profits at the expense of his journeymen, but rather tries to spread around available work. In general, the union goes out of its way to assist these contractors in finding work and maintaining their businesses because they employ union journeymen.

A second part of the union's strategy was to help its signatory contractors become more competitive with nonunion contractors. A common misconception among the public is that nonunion work has expanded because the union sector priced itself out of the market. It is true that nonunion contractors who compete with union contractors outside the residential market pay hourly wages 25 percent (in pipefitting) to 50 percent (in plumbing) less than union contractors. But this advantage is lessened because they must offer inducements to retain their skilled work force between projects. They cannot send them back to the hiring hall as union contractors do. Moreover, the wage advantage nonunion contractors enjoy is often overcome by the superior training, skill, and efficiency of the union mechanic.

Only in recent years, when nonunion contractors have been able to take advantage of union-trained skilled labor, has the efficiency advantage enjoyed by union contractors ceased to make a difference. In this context wages have become an important factor, though not the only one. Yet even if the union voluntarily lowered its wages, the nonunion sector might simply lower its and retain the advantage. Only in plumbing, where the differential is great, are wages the primary consideration.

A more important reason why nonunion contractors enjoyed a cost advantage was that their employees were not bound by jurisdictional and other work rules. They could cut costs by hiring lower-paid helpers or laborers to do unskilled parts of the job such as cutting holes in walls or moving material. Instead of hiring ten journeymen at journeymen's wages, they would hire four well-paid skilled journeymen, three mediocre workers, and three helpers. The nonunion contractors also saved by having their skilled journeymen do jobs that union journeymen could not do because it would encroach on the jurisdiction of other crafts. Finally, nonunion contractors had an advantage in being able to claim to owners that their work force would not walk off the job over jurisdictional or contract disputes.

A major attempt to remedy this lack of competitiveness came with a program called Management and Organized Labor Striving Together, or Operation MOST, established in 1976 by twenty construction unions and ten contractors' associations. The brainchild of Sam Shuman, chairman of Julian Speer Company and past president of the MCACO, MOST pledged its union participants, including Local 189, to reduce unnecessary and inefficient work practices and, perhaps most important from the contractors' point of view, cooperatively resolve jurisdictional and contract disputes. For a construction project to be termed a MOST project the unions had to agree not to halt the work by jurisdictional walk-offs, thus guaranteeing to the builder on-time completion. In return, MOST contractors agreed to use only union labor.

MOST was not only a first for the local construction industry, it was the first program of its kind in the construction industry in the United States. The MOST banner generally was reserved for large commercial and industrial projects, helping to preserve these markets for union contractors. By December 1978, $263 million in projects had been completed under MOST, and by 1985 the figure had risen to over $1 billion. As part of the overall goal of MOST in rebuilding the public image of the union sector of the industry, union craftsmen in 1980 working under MOST volunteered their time to renovate an apartment building to be used as a Ronald McDonald House for the families of children being treated for cancer and other serious illnesses at Children's Hospital. To stimulate the best quality of work and cooperation on the job, MOST construction workers selected a "craftsman of the year," the award to be given at a yearly banquet. In 1983 Local 189 member Jake Schneider received the honor.

The third prong of Local 189's response to the rise in nonunion work was the most direct. The union sought to organize the unorganized to enforce collective bargaining from the bottom up. This supplemented the top-down organizing approach that had characterized the union through the early 1970s. The initiative came from the Ohio state association of plumbers and pipefitters, which in 1974 established its former secretary Frank Burns as full-time organizer. He worked under UA international representative Bill Crellen, who had taken his position in 1972. Just signing up nonunion journeymen for the union, however, was not the answer. It would only add to the number of the men sitting on the bench. The trick was to bring in new members as part of a collectively bargained contract with a nonunion contractor.

To begin, Burns focused his efforts on organizing Croson Plumbing and Heating. Burns convinced Jim Croson to sign a prehire contract agreement that allowed the local ninety days to demonstrate to the contractor that he could get enough work under union auspices to be profitable. Meanwhile, much to Croson's discomfort, Burns had his assistant from Local 189, Bob Dyer, try to sign up his skilled journeymen. After two and a half years of these organizing efforts, Croson insisted on an election, and his men voted forty to thirteen against joining the UA. Why the defeat? Local 189's officers readily conceded that Croson treated his men well; not only did they receive comparable pay, but they had greater job security than those Local 189 members who were not steady Eddies. As one officer put it, "If all the nonunion contractors treated their men as Croson did, we wouldn't have unions. But then again, if there weren't any unions, Croson probably would not treat his men the way he does."

The defeat of the campaign against Croson demonstrated another important point: a handful of organizers, no matter how talented or aggressive or dedicated, could not reverse decades of stagnation on the organizing front. The local needed new leadership and a new attitude, not only to organize but to pursue a thorough revitalization. When members voted in Gene Brewer as business agent in 1972, they understood that need; but the local was still dominated by the much-loved Curley Steiner, or "Uncle Dudley" as he signed his reports at that time. Many younger members, who had not experienced the progress wrought by Steiner, could remember only the Group 1–Group 2 controversy and credited the charges that a clique was using favoritism in hiring hall referrals.

In 1976 two new officers were elected, who, together with a third elected in 1972, would build on Steiner's legacy and raise the local to a new plane of leadership. Gene Minix was a tall, broad-shouldered man who had ascended to the union's executive board before running for business manager on a platform of ending hiring hall favoritism and curbing the power of the clique. Minix had a low-key demeanor; he could not offer the local the charismatic leadership that Steiner had. But the local needed a different style. Minix's surface personality belied a rocklike integrity and a determination to carry out his commitments. These qualities would earn him the respect of the contractors as well as the local's members and would stabilize the union in the difficult times to come. He also carried on the Steiner tradition of close communication with the membership and a grasp of the broader issues at stake in the industry. After defeating Gene Brewer in 1976, Gene Minix became the local's third business manager in twelve years.

Running for business agent at the same time as Minix was a dynamic young man willing to "raise hell" to get the union back on its feet. Bob Dyer's intensity shone through his unyielding stare. To know Bob Dyer was to be reassured that

Gene Minix, business manager since 1976.

the fires of determination and indomitability that animated the founders of the labor movement still burned brightly. As business agent and later as Ohio State Assocation organizer, Dyer served as a bridge between those in the UA leadership on the state and national levels, who understood the need to organize come what may, and members of the local, many of whom were comfortable in their steady jobs and reluctant to take the radical measures needed to cut out the cancer eating at the union's vitals.

Charles Gronbach, elected financial secretary–treasurer in 1973, was a third component of the union's new leadership. A burly, warmhearted man deeply committed to the union, Gronbach brought to the local the highest level of competence and integrity yet achieved in financial matters. In handling hundreds of thousands of dollars, performing the accounting work for the members, and supervising an office staff of three, Gronbach, trained as a plumber, did a job that in most businesses would require a certified public accountant's degree.

How successful he had been became clear in April 1979, when an anonymous critic of the union—perhaps a disgruntled member—made charges to the U.S. Department of Labor of financial irregularities. The Federal Bureau of Investigation (FBI) launched a full-scale investigation, subpoenaing countless boxes of back records of the local and costing the membership more than $20,000 in office wages, copying costs (it took two months to copy the records), and attorney fees. Coming on the heels of federal investigations and successful prosecutions of the teamsters and the laborers unions in the city, the investigation was top-priority news in the media and seemed to confirm to the public the worst stereotype of unions as corrupt, Mafia-run institutions, out of touch with their memberships. Yet after six months of investigation by lawyers, certified public accountants, and prosecutors eager to turn up evidence of dirty dealing, the investigation was dropped on November 2 for lack of evidence. The *Columbus Dispatch* printed the FBI disclaimer on an inside page. Though the challenge to the honesty of Gronbach and the local was upsetting, the dropping of the investigation reconfirmed the integrity of the local in its financial matters. That year Gronbach ran for reelection unopposed. Two years later, the Internal Revenue Service audited the records of the local with similar results.

In 1977 the new officers—Minix, Dyer, Gronbach, and newly elected president John "Gus" Naegele—took the lead in restoring the sagging morale of the union. Minix and Naegele established a bimonthly (later semiannual) union newsletter called the *Open Line* to improve communication with the membership. The first issue in March 1977 contained an appeal from Naegele to members to start attending meetings. It also included an impassioned assessment of the state of the union from Minix:

> Each year we are slowly going down the tubes, to the nonunion element. These Contractors are coming out of the woodwork. If we as Members don't try to organize the unorganized, union craftsmen will be a thing of the past, over the next few years.
>
> Brothers, we are so unorganized and there is so much animosity among our members, we don't know the meaning of the word "Brotherhood" anymore. We don't have compassion for our Brothers like we did in the past. What have we done Brothers, giving up hope, on our Local Union? If you want strong leadership, we got to have strong Membership behind us.

John "Gus" Naegele, president from 1977 to 1979.

True to his promise, Minix and the other leaders did shake things up. The first priority was the hiring hall, the principal vehicle and symbol of fairness within the union. Because of new expectations generated in the 1960s, if the hiring hall was not perceived as being operated impartially, the feelings of brotherhood among the members would suffer and the very legitimacy of the union would be called into question.

Within the space of a year the hall underwent major changes. Formerly, contractors would call in any time in the week or day to report job openings. This practice was conducive to favoritism because all the out-of-work members could not be present at the time a job became available. Under the new system, all jobs except short-term ones were posted on Fridays and hiring took place on Mondays. To be fair to traveling members, the officers opened the hall on Saturday mornings so they could call in at their leisure to survey job openings. The union also adopted a card system to keep track of members, listing who they were working for, where, and for how long. Finally, the hall was remodeled to incorporate a large glass window so that members could see what was taking place at all times. In general, the new system removed the business agent from the process of taking and making phone calls concerning jobs and put the burden on the individual to bid to take advantage of the opportunities posted.

Minix also used his influence to swing the union solidly behind the MOST program. In the 1978 and 1980 agreements several work rules that contractors had argued were uncompetitive were modified. The required ratio of foremen to journeymen was decreased, saving the contractor money on supervision costs, and the ratio of apprentices to journeymen was increased, allowing contractors to increase the number of lower-paid workers doing unskilled tasks. As business manager, Minix met regularly over breakfast with other construction union business agents and contractors on MOST projects to resolve jurisdictional disputes amicably before they led to petty wobbles. Within the union the new leaders used their influence to urge the members to pay more attention to helping the union contractor make money on the project.

Finally, under President Jim Brennan, the union signed a special light commercial agreement with the MCACO in 1981, supplanting the residential agreement of 1971 and the statewide mechanical equipment service agreement (MES). As an incentive to contractors to hold on to that field, the agreement specified a wage for light commercial work about 60 percent of the regular journeyman's rate and a residential rate slightly lower.

The most dramatic departure from the past came in the area of organizing. Minix and Dyer wanted to shift organizing efforts from the mechanical trades to the industry as a whole by revitalizing the Building Trades Council. Since the aborted movement around the French Market, the council had degenerated into a do-nothing group. Behind the facade of friendly relations the different trades took a go-it-alone attitude, crossing each others' picket lines with regularity. This attitude extended to Local 189, for as Dyer put it, "When other [building trades] unions are involved, we seem to have a 'you did it to me, so I get you' attitude." But a new day had come. "As far as I'm concerned," wrote Dyer in the September 1977 issue of *Open Line,* "to hell with yesterday; look to tomorrow."

As soon as they were elected, both Dyer and Minix began attending council meetings to propose aggressive joint action by all the trades. They finally coalesced in 1979, when Kroger Food Stores decided to build its perishable food warehouse on the east side using nonunion labor. After Kroger refused to include union contractors on its bid list, a Local 189 picket line shut the site down. Kroger officials flew in for talks but would not allow MCACO contractors to bid on the mechanical work. With an injunction holding up picketing, Local 189 leaders finally called for an aggressive boycott. As Dyer remembers it, "by questioning their commitment to building trades unity, we just humiliated the rest of the unions into going along with us." With Dyer at the head of a citywide committee, the building trades unions returned to the direct action—without violence—they had abandoned after the French Market episode. They decided to shut down as many Kroger stores as possible.

In the winter of 1978–79 a group of one hundred Local 189 members, supported by journeymen from other trades, went into a Kroger store, filled up baskets with perishables, and left them sitting in carts in the checkout line. Kroger immediately got an injunction. The next week the union men pooled their cash and converted it into $20 bills, which they used to buy small items, quickly exhausting the store's small change. As the demonstrations grew, unions that had not sent men were confronted by Dyer and others: "Why weren't you there?" The action began to accelerate. Wives and children of the members showed up. After each series of actions, the participants held large "pep rallies" with barrels of beer on tap. After two weeks and another injunction, the unions began to buy up all the bread and other special items at a particular store, thus ruining its appeal to the average shopper. They donated the bread they had purchased to the poor.

In a later phase of the action, union members went to the bank, exchanged large bills for pennies, and loaded up a Winnebago with tens of thousands of pennies. They went from store to store, paying for large purchases in pennies. Dyer remembers: "They would go up to the clerk and slowly start counting out the pennies, '1, 2, 3,' up to a hundred or so, and then lose count—'aw hell, I'll have to start over.' We had fifteen to twenty irate customers in each line waiting and waiting, and they started leaving." It got so that when union members arrived, the store manager would announce on the public address system: "The penny people are back." All goods the union bought went to the Open Food Pantry charity.

Finally, Kroger relented; it would build with union workers. On March 15, 1979, representatives from building trades councils in Ohio and five other states met in Columbus to discuss common problems, such as those with Kroger, and analyze the tactics employed. The same month, Gene Minix was elected president of the Building Trades Council, a position he would hold for a decade. An exultant Dyer reported in the union's newsletter:

> Brothers, I cannot put in words the gratitude that is due you, the people who gave up your time to help in this uphill fight. You have taken a big bite out of the A.B.C.'s, but please don't believe this is the time to quit. This is the turning point. You have taken on one of the multi-million dollar giants and won. The rest will be easier. For the first time in years the Columbus Building Trades Council has laid its internal problems aside and united. Brothers, no individual building trades union can survive and combat the nonunion element without the support of the other building trades unions.

The union used the tactics tried on Kroger with success against K-Mart in 1981, when it departed from its previous build-union policy. Armed with pounds of pennies, members of the union and their families bought up scores of K-Mart toys, creating long lines at the store. Afterward, the union donated some of the toys to a local community house for Christmas presents. They gave away the rest to three to four hundred orphans and poor children at a big Christmas party at the union's hall. K-Mart soon relented.

But the main focus of organizing was aimed at nonunion contractors. Since 1977 Dyer had been Frank Burns's right-hand man in organizing work. They had identified nonunion contractors in the area, whom Dyer would visit, explain the benefits of union labor, and offer to sign a basic collective bargaining agreement. If that didn't work, the union swung into job actions: organizing, picketing, and boycotting.

The effort gained its first major success with the Favret Company, a sixty-year-old HVAC contracting company employing forty-two journeymen. In early 1981 the union won a National Labor Relations Board election that obligated the employer to bargain with the union in good faith. After three months of bad faith bargaining, in which Favret's intransigence was encouraged by the ABC, Favret employees voted to strike. By the fourth week of the walkout the union had placed over half the workers in temporary jobs with friendly contractors in Local 189's jurisdiction, thus enabling the men to cover their strike costs. Toward the end of the sixth week, Favret advertised for strikebreakers, offering wages higher than those he had offered the local at the bargaining table. Over the following two

*Bob Dyer has organized in Columbus since 1972. He is
currently Ohio state organizer.*

days the union mobilized 120 men, many from the unemployed list and even
members who gave up a day of work, in addition to Favret employees. According
to Dyer, "All realized at this point that the strike had developed into a head to
head fight with the nonunion ABC Contractors who were supporting Favret
Company, knowing they might be next." After two days of what Jim Favret
admitted was "impressive union solidarity," he sent word that he would sign an
interim light commercial (including MES) agreement, which he did on August 5.
Two months later the union swore in thirty-two new brothers.

But that was not the only tactic. When one general contractor (Setterlin)
refused to dissolve his nonunion operation, a business agent for the ironworkers
bought a rat's costume and followed him around in an antique convertible. Dyer
adopted this tactic and first used it with a small nonunion contractor in Zanesville,

following him around town on the back of a flatbed truck, advertising his nonunion hiring practices to the local townspeople. It became a major issue in the town, with signs in local stores reading "The Rat Is Welcome Here" or "Rat: Stay Away." Within two weeks the contractor signed up, and there were no hard feelings. "Ralph the Rat," as he came to be known, was then pressed into service with success in Local 189 organizing campaigns.

Altogether, the three-pronged strategy of encouraging members to become contractors, using mass pressure to organize and keep builders from going nonunion, and especially the attempt to help union contractors become more competitive paid real dividends to the union. By all accounts, the trend toward nonunion construction was halted and perhaps somewhat reversed during the last half of the 1970s and early 1980s. A survey done by Herbert R. Northrup in his book *Open Shop Construction Revisited,* published in 1984, concluded that in Columbus the construction industry had bucked the national trend of a rising nonunion share of construction work. According to Northrup, the union share of new work was at least 50 percent as measured by value. The book gave major credit to the MOST programs for improving productivity and eliminating jurisdictional disputes. Sam Shuman, MOST's first chairman, confirms this conclusion, citing the popularity of MOST with builders because it guaranteed on-time completion of their projects. Gene Minix called MOST "a damned good program."

Yet MOST did not continue, and the trend away from union construction resumed in the 1980s.

The Dismal 1980s

MOST received two body blows in 1982 and 1983. The most important was the defection of several general contractors from the program. The trend began with Setterlin Construction, a supporter of MOST, which went completely nonunion. Then a host of other general contractors doing many of the big commercial downtown jobs as well as industrial work began to open up nonunion operations along with their union ones. They had gone "double-breasted." Several mechanical contractors also opened up nonunion subsidiaries under different names and at different offices.

The double-breasted contractors thought they had the best of both worlds. If they needed skilled men on a high-efficiency, tight-deadline job, they tapped the building trades unions' hiring halls. But if the job had no such quality or time requirements, they would subcontract it out to cheaper "rat" shops.

The unions wanted MOST to continue, but it was impossible to designate a job for MOST if the contractor was doing nonunion work on the side. And by the late 1980s there were only two or three prominent general contractors in Columbus who were not double-breasted. The result was that the impact of MOST on the construction industry in Columbus diminished steadily.

From the contractors' point of view, what hurt MOST was the return of walkouts to an industry that had been strike-free for almost a decade. In June 1982 Local 189, together with the ironworkers, walked out over the size of a wage increase. President Jim Brennan explained the issue: "We had pretty well agreed to concessions on apprentice ratios and travel pay for work in outlying areas that we could live with if the wage proposal was in line. It was not and we went on strike June 1."

To contractors the strike for a $1.50 wage increase over each of two years of the contract broke a local pattern in which the different trades would agree to similar increases for two-year periods. "Pattern bargaining" avoided what they called "leapfrogging" or "whipsawing" in which the different construction unions vied for the highest settlement. To contractors sitting on the fence between operating union or nonunion, the strike boded a return to walkouts and undermined their faith in MOST. Of course, Local 189 had gone for a decade without large wage increases and wanted to catch up with the sharply rising prices of the late 1970s. The increases seemed especially justified because the union offered concessions in other areas. Moreover, the union had never accepted local pattern bargaining and had tried to salvage MOST by refusing to strike MOST jobs. But the damage to relations with some contractors was irreparable.

With MOST withering on the vine, the union's best hope lay in organizing. Yet here too the union suffered setbacks. By 1980 many local members were unhappy with the organizing results of Frank Burns, Charlie Smithers, and Bob Dyer. They complained that the organizers were bringing men into the local without also bringing their employers under contract. The upshot was that there were more members on the bench competing for the same number of jobs. This was not the fault of the organizers. If they could not convince a contractor to sign a collective bargaining agreement on his own volition (top-down organizing), they had to try to "card" his employees (bottom-up organizing). Once signed up, the shop's key people had to be promised union membership if the employer would not sign a contract and instead retaliated against them for joining the union.

National Labor Relations Board rules may have prohibited such discrimination, but it was difficult to win a complaint against an employer for offering more overtime hours to his "loyal" nonunion employee than to his "disloyal" union employee. Indeed, this became normal practice for nonunion contractors acting on the advice of ABC. Even if the union won an NLRB election, the contractors would drag out the process of negotiating a contract and move to decertify the union. Over an extended period of time it became difficult to convince prospective union members to stick by the union.

Even worse, the Taft-Hartley amendments to the National Labor Relations Act, which had largely lain dormant for two decades after their enactment in 1947, were now coming back to haunt the unions in numerous ways. Officials of building trades unions could not use sanctions to influence their members to respect the picket lines of other trades. This was a secondary boycott outlawed under Taft-Hartley. Of course, it was legal for members to respect a picket line on their own volition, but the nonunion contractors had a way around this. When general contractors mixed nonunion mechanical trades journeymen with union building trades journeymen on the same job, Local 189 found it difficult to shut the operation down by picketing because contractors would set up a two-gate system, one for union and one for nonunion employees. It was illegal to picket the union gate for that was a secondary boycott, but it would be futile to picket the nonunion gate. The prohibition against secondary boycotts was also used as the basis for injunctions against the union for trying to shut down builders such as Kroger's and K-Mart, who built nonunion. In sum, it became a difficult and tricky business to use building trades solidarity—what little existed—to organize the unorganized.

Because the NLRB was unworkable, a cruel dilemma faced the union: it could either take in nonunion mechanics and increase unemployment or try to convince nonunion employers to sign contracts without exerting any real pressure. The difficulty of organizing was made worse because no strong constituency within the union backed organizing. Those with steady jobs tended not to want to rock the boat. Those who were without steady jobs and dominated the union meetings were fearful that bottom-up organizing would result in intensified competition for scarce work. A vocal group of members in the union were unhappy that any organizing was being done. They pointed out that even when brought under contract, small contractors often went bankrupt, and they complained that organizing Favret had not improved employment possibilities for most journeymen because the company offered only service work. So obstinate had the opposition grown that Bob Dyer, who had replaced Burns in 1981 as state organizer, shifted his organizing focus away from Columbus to locales in Ohio where he enjoyed greater support.

Unfortunately, these setbacks were not the only ones faced by the local in the early 1980s. No one knows how many Local 189 members voted for Ronald Reagan for president in 1980 and again in 1984, but informed estimates are that a large minority—on top of the 30 percent of the membership that are registered Republicans—went against the recommendations of UA and local officers and did so. By 1988 the members apparently had had enough of Reagan. A confidential poll of ninety-nine members present at a union meeting two weeks before the November election found that with only four exceptions union members supported Democrats for state and federal offices (locally, union officers normally recommend that members split their votes among Republicans and Democrats).

But the damage had already been done. Ronald Reagan, in his zeal to deregulate business, did his best to undermine the NLRB with antiunion appointees; he gutted enforcement of health and safety on the job by the Occupational Safety and Health Administration (OSHA) and crushed an ill-advised air traffic controllers' strike in 1981, firing over 11,500 highly skilled union members. The president's actions signaled full speed ahead to union busters all over the nation. In the seven years after the destruction of the Professional Air Traffic Controllers' Organization (PATCO), the membership of organized labor all over the United States plummeted. Never since the 1920s had the morale and reputation of labor in America been at a lower ebb than under the administration of Ronald Reagan. Of special interest to building trades unions during these years was the attempt in Congress to repeal or at least reduce the effectiveness of the Davis-Bacon (prevailing wage) Act.

Compounding the legacy of inflation from the late 1970s, the economic policy of the Reagan administration brought prodigious federal budget deficits that induced the Federal Reserve Board to raise interest rates to fight inflation. As a result, the economy fell into decline and sectors such as construction that were heavily dependent on credit were brought to their knees. The recession of 1981–82, the worst since the 1930s bringing 10 percent unemployment nationwide, was felt intensely by Columbus construction workers. In 1982 almost three hundred Local 189 members were unemployed, about 30 percent of the union's active members. This situation worsened in 1983, which Charles Gronbach, writing in the *Open Line,* called "the worst year I have known in my 27 years in the local. . . . Many of our members have expired all their unemployment benefits, including federal extensions and have insufficient weeks for new claims [a minimum of twenty weeks of work was required]." In 1984, though the nation had recovered from the recession, the union slipped further into the doldrums with a monthly average of 40 percent of its members sitting on the bench during the year.

The younger members were hardest hit by unemployment. Many were married with small children and were trying to buy homes. Perhaps even worse was the blow that extended unemployment delivered to their pride and self-respect. "Why am I out of work?" they asked each morning as they faced themselves in the mirror: "I *want* to work; I'm not a loafer." To anyone who would listen, they would vow defiantly: "I'm as good a mechanic as anybody." But the self-doubts inevitably took their toll.

Unemployment, double-breasted contractors, a hostile political environment, disunity in the building trades, an inability to organize, and a rising share of new work taken by nonunion contractors were hammer blows to the union during the first half of the 1980s. What could the union do? Ever ready with new ideas, state organizer Bob Dyer offered the provocative idea that the union go into business for itself as a "Union Cooperative." The goal, as outlined in a memo distributed to members in 1983, was to regain the light commercial and residential field that "has not been bid by union contractors" and "to employ members who are now or will be unemployed." Shares would be available to union members only, and the number of shares a member could hold would be limited. The cooperative would be managed by three retired members receiving $1 a year.

Unlike the cooperative started by the local during the 1904 strike, the 1983 Union Cooperative would not have attempted to compete with and ultimately displace the MCACO contractors with whom the union was bound by collective bargaining. Bidding by the cooperative would have been limited to fields dominated by nonunion contractors. Why not go into business on their own, thought many members. After all, union members have experience, expertise, and long-term commitment to the industry. In this sense the cooperative idea was a logical extension of the policy enunciated in the early 1970s of encouraging members to go into business for themselves.

After being assured by legal counsel that the idea was feasible, the union scheduled a meeting on March 20, 1984, to set the plan into motion. At that meeting the cooperative gathered only about $23,000 of the $50,000 needed for start-up capital in the form of pledges. The inability to secure the services of retired members capable of effectively managing the cooperative turned out to be an even greater problem. As a result, the idea was tabled indefinitely.

Meanwhile, the desperate circumstances faced by the union forced it to pay more attention to proposals by the contractors to enhance their competitiveness. At the top of its list of negotiating proposals from the late 1970s into the 1980s, the MCACO asked for restoration of lower-paid helpers to perform unskilled work such as unloading material and cutting holes in walls. Another proposal by contractors would allow them, through various means, to circumvent the hiring hall's first-in, first-out rule to secure the journeymen *they* wanted.

The union strenuously resisted both proposals. The idea of helpers, though adopted by several UA locals elsewhere, found no support in Local 189. Certainly, lower-paid helpers would make the contractors more competitive, but the union had no faith that the new jobs gained would outnumber the skilled jobs lost to less-skilled helpers. As for circumventing the hiring hall, it was unthinkable that the union would consent to dismantle what it had fought so hard to attain. Undermining the hiring hall would sanction an informal blacklist of those on the bench who might incur the ill will of contractors for standing up for union rules. Contractors often called these hall people "damned troublemakers." As one member put it, if that ever came to pass, many "good union men, even skilled union men would never work."

A host of other collective bargaining issues remained, on each of which there was some room for compromise. The first major contract giveback came over the issue of travel pay. During this period, MCACO contractors found themselves at a competitive disadvantage vis-à-vis national contractors operating under the UA's national contract, which had no provision for travel pay. When the MCACO demanded a $3.60 wage reduction in 1984, the union decided instead to give up travel pay within its jurisdiction—then figured at $.25 per mile—with the exception of transfer from one job to another during the working day. They also allowed the percentage of journeyman's wages received by new apprentices to be significantly reduced in steps of 45 percent (year 1), 55 percent (year 2), 70 percent (year 3), and 85 percent (year 4) as stipulated in the 1982 contract to a flat rate, which amounted to steps of 30, 42, 52, and 73 percent in the 1984 contract.

Apprenticeship took another blow. Looking for ways to assist the contractors in reducing costs, the union agreed to cut $120,000 a year used to pay apprentices to attend training classes during work hours. The JAC replaced the day classes with night classes, which it required apprentices to attend for four hours, two nights a week.

In August 1984, two months after the contract had been ratified, the patience of many members over the givebacks reached the exploding point. Many union members had just returned from a demonstration against Mead Corporation in Chillicothe. Those who had gone were largely the out-of-work members, and many of them had had too much to drink. Upon returning to the hall, they were in an angry mood. During the meeting members shouted at each other and exchanged heated words, voicing the old charge of "sellout." President Dick Patterson took most of the heat, even though the contract had been negotiated by five members of the union bargaining committee other than himself (including Gene Minix) and ratified by 70 percent of the membership. After failing to restore order, he turned the meeting over to Vice-President Mike Zack and left the hall. At the first meeting in September, after a verbal exchange between another member of the bargaining committee and Greg Murphy, Patterson felt that his presence was creating dissension in the local and resigned his office (he retained his position as apprenticeship coordinator).

Bob Meredith, elevated to the presidency in a special election in November, paid more attention to the currents agitating the members. When the contractors demanded a 20 percent wage reduction in 1985, he led a strike in June. Unfortunately, he had not given the contractors sixty days' notice as required by federal law and was forced to bring the members back to avoid a court injunction. After he gave formal notice, negotiations resumed, resulting in twenty-one-cent and twenty-five-cent wage increases over the following two years, which were subsequently applied to health and welfare.

Unable to get wage reductions or helpers, contractors resorted to other cost-reduction measures. Companies such as Julian Speer began in the 1980s to remove work on the job to its fabrication shop. This process was facilitated by a more liberal article in the collective bargaining agreement offered by the union in the 1970s. For example, plumbing fixtures, which formerly were fabricated on the job by plumbers, are now assembled more economically inside the company's "fab" shop. Julian Speer also attempted to do as much welding as possible in the fab shop by micro-wire welding rather than on the job by "stick" welding. All work continues to be done by union labor (Local 189 members will not install any material unless it bears the union label).

Beginning in the last half of 1985, the amount of work available to journeymen gradually increased from the low level of 1984. But the average number of hours worked in the local between 1985 and 1988 still stagnated about 18 percent below the level worked during the 1979–81 period. With nonunion work still slowly but seemingly inexorably spreading into the commercial and industrial sectors, the union decided in 1988 to try to reduce the pressure on union contractors to cut wages and to increase their incentive not to abdicate less profitable jobs to nonunion contractors. The union called the new scheme the Targeted Jobs Program and modeled it on the experience of the Columbus International Brotherhood of Electrical Workers (electricians) Local 683.

The Targeted Jobs Program created a fund out of a 2 percent dues increase levied on Local 189 members to allow for lower bids by MCACO contractors when in competition with nonunion contractors. Thus if an MCACO contractor decided that he needed to pay his fitters from Local 189 20 percent less in wages to be competitive on a particular job, he would submit a request to Local 189 to target the job, the number of hours to be worked, and the wage rate. Upon the union's approval, he would receive from the fund the difference between the collectively bargained wage rate and the lower rate multiplied by the number of hours worked, assuming the contractor won the bid. The Targeted Jobs Program went into effect in October 1988 and has been moderately successful, with the union obtaining about half of the first one hundred jobs it targeted over a year and a half. Very few of the jobs won under the Targeted Jobs Program—mostly nonplumbing jobs—would have gone to the union without the union subsidy.

The strategy of working more closely with the MCACO to enhance union contractors' competitiveness also paid dividends in the efforts of the Joint Apprenticeship Committee to improve training. Apprenticeship programs and the resulting skilled, efficient labor may be the most important edge unionized contractors have over nonunion contractors. Since 1984, a new JAC, consisting of Dave Maxwell, Ron Graves, Fred Scolieri, Steve Justice, and contractors' representatives Mike Shuman, Joe Salyer, and Paul Gronbach, has funded expanded classroom space, hired more instructors, increased instruction time for apprentices from 144 to 216 hours, and increased the number of training classes for journeymen.

The union has also worked at improving its public image. Based on its traditional concern for public safety, the union, led by business agent Bill Steinhauser, combined with local union contractors, who donated service trucks and tools, to organize the Heats-On program for the 1989–90 winter season. After being filmed for television, 230 Local 189 volunteers inspected the homes of 209 Columbus senior citizens to check the safety of heating and cooling equipment and piping. They installed smoke detectors and thermostats donated by local businesses and made minor repairs free of charge. Heats-On will be an ongoing union-contractor program.

Meanwhile, Bob Dyer returned to the Columbus area after six years organizing elsewhere in the state. Working with Bob Meredith, who became business agent in 1987, Dyer achieved notable success in organizing and removing the skilled labor of a leading nonunion firm in the area.

The Targeted Jobs Program, improved apprenticeship training and public relations, and renewed organizing are important steps in promoting the unionized sector of the industry. But the tide has not yet been turned, as is reflected in stagnating wages and the local's unwillingness since 1985 to risk a strike. Under Presidents Fred Scolieri and Pat Ferry the union funneled most of its increased compensation into shoring up its health and welfare program, which had been verging on insolvency because of spiraling increases in health care costs. Members' hourly contributions to health and welfare have more than doubled since 1986, while wages increased only from $19.55 to $20.00 an hour in the 1988–91 contract. The stagnation in wages during most of the 1980s is highlighted by the statistic that from June 1, 1983, through May 31, 1991, wages increased only $.91, an average of six-tenths of 1 percent per year, by far the worst record during the postwar period. That figure translated into a continuous decline in the purchasing power of journeymen's wages given the average yearly inflation rate of about 4 percent.

During this period the union also modified its hiring hall procedure, once again to suit the contractors. Confronted by strong pressure on the contractors by the EEOC to increase the number of black journeymen by establishing a separate hiring list for blacks, the union and the MCACO compromised to head off such a list, which would have greatly worsened racial tensions within the union. The 1988 contract allowed a contractor to pick one member from the hiring hall anywhere on the list as long as he picked two other members from the top of the list.

By 1989, Local 189 had lost virtually all residential construction, had less than

Pat Ferry, president from 1988 to 1991.

5 percent of plumbing in all markets, and controlled only 25 percent of the commercial market. Only in industrial work was the union still strong, holding over half the market, but even here the local was slipping. More and more members were forced to ask themselves with anguish questions that would have been unthinkable two decades ago: Will the union be around in the next century? Can I advise my son or daughter to be a union member in a trade in which they may sit on the bench for long periods?

Illuminating answers to these questions have come from contractors. One of the union's biggest nemeses in the past, Jim Croson, believes that if unions did not exist, wages would fall to levels at which it would be impossible to attract high-quality journeymen to the trade. Not only would union employers suffer, but, he admits, so would nonunion contractors such as himself. Most nonunion contractors, in fact, rely on the union sector both to train their skilled work force and to maintain a high wage level—which these contractors undercut slightly to gain their advantage. Sam Shuman, a union employer and member of the MCACO, also thinks that unions will continue to be viable in the industry. Not only do they develop and maintain the skilled labor necessary to do the important commercial and industrial jobs, but they prevent the average journeyman from being taken advantage of by unscrupulous employers.

But unionists cannot take too much comfort from this assessment, for to say that unions will continue to exist leaves unanswered a question almost as important: How much of the market will they control? Will the union in Columbus retreat to the margins of the industry, content to do the highly skilled industrial work, or will it regain the dominance it enjoyed during the golden age of construction unionism during the 1940s, 1950s, and 1960s? Will the union shrivel into a small club of highly skilled mechanics, or will it once again open its ranks to all the journeymen who prove their skill by their ability to retain employment in the trade? If it be the latter, the union will need to make major modifications in its attitude toward organizing. Or it may have to take a chance on what was once unthinkable: large wage cuts and the employment of helpers to improve the competitiveness of their employers. A more drastic remedy, rarely discussed openly and requiring the cooperation of other building trades unions, would be the consolidation of the different crafts into four or six general construction unions so as to end jurisdictional disputes and enhance union contractors' flexibility on the job. Whatever route the union takes, superior apprenticeship and journeyman training will continue to be the union's ultimate weapon.

It is possible that the 1990s will be a decade of decision for members of Local 189 and the mechanical contractors who employ them. In this pivotal decade the plumbers and pipefitters will rely more than ever before on qualities that have sustained their union for a full century: a pride in their workmanship as mechanics and a commitment to union solidarity.

6. E Pluribus Unum:
Faces in the Union

A union is many things at once. It is an economic organization providing a service to its members by securing for them job opportunities and proper wages, benefits, and working conditions. In the case of building trades unions it is also a craft organization striving to preserve craft pride by maintaining and upgrading the skills of its members. But a union is also a living human community. Like the motto of the United States—E Pluribus Unum—a union attempts to create unity out of diversity. Throughout much of its history the labor movement successfully united white male workers of different nationalities. Today, it is called upon to do more: build a community uniting in solidarity working people of different races and genders.

The following interviews of Local 189 members attest to the continuance of barriers in achieving the goal of full solidarity. But they also make clear that a common ground exists that can and does unite a diverse membership. The members whose voices are heard in this chapter were selected for their diversity. A white male union veteran provides over five decades of perspective on the local; a black male plumber from a nonunion background discusses his experience with discrimination; a white female pipefitter speaks of how she has adapted to being a part of a union that for almost a century was limited to a "brotherhood"; a popular president talks about how he became an officer; a white male union activist reflects on what the union has meant to him personally; and a young apprentice from a Hispanic background offers his insights on what being an apprentice is like. In each case the inverviewees discuss how their commitment to their union and their trade has shaped their life.

Francis Wolfe

Francis Wolfe, seventy-three years old and known to his peers affectionately as "Franny," does not have the appearance of an old man. Unlike some journeymen, who have been disabled by injury or disease, Wolfe is physically trim, vigorous, alert, and thoughtful. His accurate memory and dispassionate, balanced judgments about the union's past were an important source in the writing of chapters 4 and 5 of this book.

I was born in Morgan County in 1916, and my parents moved to Columbus when I was five. We were poor, but we didn't know it. During the Depression everyone was poor. I graduated from North High School in 1934. My father was a laborer employed in various and sundry jobs; he grabbed what he could get. He was killed in a construction accident in 1934. College was out of the question; we had virtually no money. So I drifted around and worked at odd jobs—I pumped gas, I sold Coca-Cola door to door on commission, and ended up working for a roofing firm. My sister was a stenographer for Huffman-Wolfe, and through her influence I got a job driving a truck for them. In the course of that work I met union mechanics. Although I had no idea about unionism, everyone belonged to the union. I impressed a man named Ted Slick on a job in Springfield, Ohio. For some reason he took an interest in me and suggested that I get into a trade. Frankly, I had no interest in it. I'm nineteen years old and I'm driving a truck! I'm a wheel! I don't want to get down there and wallow in the mud with those fellows.

But the boss said either I go down and work at the trade or I get let go. He had no more work for me. So I registered with Local 189 as a helper. I became Slick's helper. I was sort of indentured to him. Where he went, I went. This went on pretty regularly from 1936 until 1939. I was learning the trade all this time. The defense effort had begun to build at this time. Prior to this time it had been very difficult to get into our union. You had to have a father or brother or somebody in the union; you didn't walk in off the street. I was associated with the union back then but was not allowed to be a member. We helpers had a little ticket and once a month we came down to the hall to get our ticket punched. The union was rather a cliquish thing. There were no equal opportunity statutes. But when government work began to get geared up, we ran short of men. An effort was made to recruit people into the local for the first time since before the Depression. One of the first places they looked was the helpers—there were

Francis Wolfe

about fifteen to twenty helpers. I took the examination and got into the local. It wasn't my idea to become a steamfitter, I just went with the flow.

Early on, I didn't care for the work at all and I would never in the world have suspected that it would become a career. My boyhood ambition was to become a motion picture news photographer. But there was absolutely no opportunity back then. I got into the pipefitting trade to make a living. This was a job, and I did it. In retrospect I realize I had mechanical aptitude, but I didn't realize it then. I was conscientious in working at it. That doesn't make any sense; usually when you don't like something you don't do a good job at it, but I did! I call myself the world's most successful failure. I made a very good living. I had a very good family life; I raised two kids and put them through college, and my kids are both successful and I've had nice homes and a nice living, so how could I complain? In retrospect I probably did like it, but back then I kept telling myself I didn't.

I've met a lot of interesting people and seen a lot of interesting places. I worked quite a bit in the foundry shops—at Buckeye Steel Castings and other places—putting in process piping. I've learned how freeze-dried coffee was made; I've seen how millions of loaves of bread were made by huge machines at bakeries. We worked in office buildings, paper mills, aluminum plants, and hospitals and learned how these institutions were run. I came up with a vast storehouse of immensely fascinating knowledge that the average person is not familiar with at all.

I've had a lot of interesting experiences. You want to hear something humorous? Once I was working in a hospital and I had to dress in a surgeon's gown and mask whenever I went into a certain room to work. One time I was walking down the hall wearing the gown and mask and carrying my toolbox with the saw and pliers and everything, and I walked past a woman who was lying on a table about to be sedated for surgery. She looked at me and said, "I sincerely hope you're not the doctor."

I was four years in the navy, 1942–46. I was in the North Atlantic and then was transferred to a repair ship in the Mediterranean. Then I went on to the Marshall Islands in the Pacific. I had some GI credit coming and I could have gone back to school. But my rationale was that it would take me four years to get out and another ten for my earning potential to get back to where it was being a journeyman pipefitter. Looking back, I had it pretty good. I was rarely hurt and rarely out of work. By the time the economy slowed down, I was pretty well established. I never had any problems with unemployment.

Over the years I appreciated the impact that the union was having on me. I realized that had I not belonged to the union, I wouldn't have been in the position to travel around the country, get into all these interesting jobs, learn all these interesting things, and meet all these fine, for the most part, people. After I retired, I maintained my interest. We had an election last Saturday, and I worked all day at the polls. I've been retired since 1981. Right at the end I did get laid off and I had to get an out-of-town job.

Eventually, I became a foreman and a supervisor and this taught me how to get along with people and how to get things done. That's been tremendously beneficial to me. I've rarely met anyone I can't get along with. One of the things peculiar to the construction trades is that today you're a boss, tomorrow you're a mechanic. So you learn not to antagonize the other guy because tomorrow you may be working for him. And you've got to make money for the boss or you won't be working. We've all got an oar in the same boat. There was a period in the late 1960s when we lost sight of this, but in the early 1970s it came back to us.

The first part of my career I wasn't married. There was a little bit of prestige to being on the road. I had a little bit of glamour in the eyes of the local gentry, if you know what I mean. Here's this guy, he's come in; he's running the job down at General Motors; he's from Columbus, Ohio; he travels around the country and does all this. And I liked all this! I could scoop in girls by the dozen [laughs]; had quite a bit of money. What's not to like?

I was married in '51. At the time I was working on a job at the Bethlehem Steel Company in Baltimore. I was almost finished with the job when I came home and got married. I got married on a Saturday and took my wife back with me on Sunday. Our honeymoon suite was a compartment on the Spirit of St. Louis going to Baltimore. I was down there a few weeks, came home for a short time, and got a job in Trenton, New Jersey, with U.S. Steel. That time I took my wife with me. My wife would go out and get a job. She was an accountant. I bought a house in Columbus, but we didn't live in it. After two or three years we had a son, and the three of us went on the road. I bought a trailer—it was becoming difficult to find furnished apartments. In two or three more years, our daughter came along and the boy was old enough to go to school. Gradually, the out-of-town work diminished for me. There wasn't much of it anymore.

It's my opinion that we have the best mechanics in the country right here in Columbus. I believe it. There is nothing going on in the trade in this country that we don't have somebody in this local that can do it. Look at us: we've built a major brewery, all sorts of major manufacturing plants—Fisher Guide, Mead Paper. There's nothing going in the country that isn't going on in this city!

A lot of our people travel a lot. It depends a great deal on what the conditions are here. It's not unusual for us to have two or three hundred men working out of town. During the period of the Alaska pipeline a lot of our people went up there. Some of our people haven't come back yet! This is one of the benefits of belonging to the UA. If you can't find a job here, you've got the whole United States. Your network and a telephone call can get you a job. Our business agents are constantly in touch with other locals. Or you can hear things such as: I've got a cousin who lives in Pittsburgh and there's a big GM plant and they're hiring five hundred guys and so you go down to your business agent and have him call up. You've got a big pool of jobs to draw from. There's never been a day in my life that I've worried about getting work. I've seldom had down time. The union has given me a good living. My daughter helps control the budget at Ohio State University and my son has a fine job at Bell Labs (AT&T).

I get a great deal of enjoyment associating with the people on the job. I enjoy knowing them. I feel good talking to them. I talk to the old guys about the old days, and I tell the young guys how easy they have it [laughs]. I get social security plus two separate union pensions. I'm doing very well right now.

This is a great union hall. I don't know of another place in the country that has as nice a place as this. We have a bang-up picnic at the zoo and occasional banquets during the year, a dance, and television football parties and social gatherings. It's sort of like a nice club. I belong to a church, but I have no other social affiliations. When I feel the need to socialize, I come down here. I'm an old guy and everybody knows me, and maybe I have some privileges that others don't have. I can go into Charlie's [financial secretary-treasurer Gronbach] office and say hello and talk; I don't make a pest of myself. But I like to think I'm welcome to come in here every time I want to. A lot of the older workers and retired people appreciate this facet of the organization. Keep it in balance. This is a business office and I have no right to interrupt any operation, but I don't see anything really wrong with it. A lot of people hang out in the social room with a coffee pot, playing cards and talking. Some are out of work and retired or semiretired. A great many of our members keep their name on the out-of-work list and dues paid, and if something comes along that they particularly want to work at, or a foreman or journeyman they want to work with, they take it. They don't really have to work.

The union has allowed me to occupy a position of respect in society. I'm not some bum. As my father told me before he died, "Whatever you do, learn to do something definite, so you'll know what kind of work you're out of." I have done that, and that's a good feeling. Friends that I have who work in factories—General Motors Fisher Guide—they're continually under threat of getting laid off. What are they going to do? They've been sticking this bolt in this hole for fifteen years. I have a trade and an organization backing me up. Being unemployed never worried me one minute.

Albert Kirk

Albert Kirk is one of the few black union members of Local 189. Of medium build, with close-cropped hair and a mustache, Al radiates an air of calm and friendly self-confidence. Though starting out nonunion, he has been a union journeyman plumber for the past fifteen years.

When I was twelve or thirteen years old I started working weekends and summer vacations with my dad. My father, Christopher Jack Kirk, was one of the first blacks out of five or six to hold a master's plumbing license in the city of Columbus. In the late 1940s one out of that group went on to be the chief plumbing inspector for the city of Columbus. It wasn't easy because at that time the inspector didn't want to give the test to a black.

I don't know if my dad ever tried to get into the union. One time, when I was working for a nonunion contractor, he asked me if I wanted to work for the union. I said, "I'm doing OK right now; I don't really think they would give me a job anyway," so I didn't worry about it. This was about the time that the brewery started, and they were hiring anyone they could get with any knowledge of plumbing and pipefitting at all.

My work is my life, really. It's the only thing that I really know. Plumbing is just a part of me. I've grown up around it all my life. At first, when I was a kid I didn't think I would ever really stay in it, but the more that I did, the more knowledge I gained. Everything was digging ditches with a shovel and a pick; that's the way we did it back then. You cut the pipe with a hammer and chisel; we didn't have a pipe machine; oil it with one hand and push down on the handle with the other hand—the hardest possible way of doing it—that's the way we did it. At

Albert Kirk

first, it was hard to get used to, but I got accustomed to it. I enjoy it, I love the trade, and I wouldn't think about doing anything else.

The different materials and techniques are changing every couple of years so it keeps you interested; you're always learning. Mostly what I did before was plumbing, but now I'm doing refrigeration; I work with fitters; I'm working now over at the main library where they're doing renovation work. I'm working doing the fitting for the welder in the boiler room; it's my first boiler room; but I'm enjoying it; it's a challenge and a new experience for me; I make mistakes sometimes; I work them out and just keep on going.

When I worked nonunion the fact that they didn't really care about quality was one of my biggest hangups. They just wanted the job done. They wanted speed more than quality and accuracy. That's something I've always prided myself in: trying to do the best job I possibly could; I won't say the job's perfect, but it's the best I can do. And I'm gonna be happy with it when I walk away from it. In other words, if they give me enough time to do the job right, it'll be right, and I'll be proud of it and so will anybody who sees it. If it's not right, then I won't be happy with it and nobody else will be happy with it and I'm going to be ashamed. And I don't want to be ashamed of nothing. So I always try to do the best I can.

The first job I had when I left my dad was with Wood's Plumbing, and I was the only minority there. I applied for a job as a plumber's helper. The man who was running the company said I couldn't go out as a helper because he didn't think people would accept me coming into their homes. I started as a *shop boy* making a dollar and a half an hour. I worked there three and a half years, and when I left, I was still making a dollar and a half an hour. During that time I went from being a shop boy to running the cash register, to driving trucks, going out helping on the jobs, actually doing plumbing, running a backhoe machine, and they never give me even a one-cent raise. I asked him about a raise. He said, *"All you people* think when you start learning the trade is that you deserve a raise."* The answer to my question was no. Just be glad you have a job. I knew it was time to move on.

The next and last nonunion job I had was with A. L. Wing, for about five and a half years between 1967 and 1973. When I first went in there, I was the only minority. They probably had fifty to sixty people at times. They weren't too sure about my experience and abilities, but they grew to respect me and I grew to respect them. It was a good growing experience. I could remember the owner of the company—his son had asked me if I could get a license so he asked his dad,

"Why don't you give Al a codebook so he can study for his test?" He said, "OK, I'll give him one," but he didn't do anything. So a couple of weeks later he asked him again and he said he had an old one and he would sell it to me. I don't know, but I had a bad feeling. I don't know if it was racial or what, but he didn't have anything to say to me at all; he wasn't friendly at all, just standoffish.

I got the book, studied, and passed the test the first time so I went and talked to him about a raise; that comes after getting your license. I was making about $3 an hour; I wanted a dollar raise; he said fifty cents; so he tried me out to see what I could do. The first job he put me on was his apartment building off Cleveland Avenue. During that job, with him coming out and checking on me and everything, his attitude totally changed. He grew to like and respect me through my work, and he could see I wasn't cheating him; I was there every day. I wasn't taking long lunches; I was giving him eight hours' work for eight hours' pay. The man grew to like me; I mean we really got close. His son and I got to be real close friends, and he worked under me as my helper.

It's always kind of been that way with me anyway when I go in. Usually I'm the only minority there. A lot of time when I go in, the people are really cold and standoffish; I don't know if it's the difference in the race or what, but once I'm there long enough and they know me and see that I'm a hard worker, they usually loosen up and we get to be friends.

I had it made pretty well where I was nonunion; I was liked and was making good money. It's totally different out here working in the union. [In 1973] I was called by the EEOC about a job with the union. It was a big step. I did a lot of thinking about it; I really wasn't sure. I knew that in the union there was a great deal of pride and, like I said, when I worked nonunion the main thing with them was just get it in, and as long as it looks halfway decent we'll let it go. But in the union it has to be right. I mean that they want quality work; they want top-rated work; and that's what makes me feel good about being in the union. It's doing a good job; that's what everybody expects, that's what everybody looks for. It's just a good feeling when you do a good job. I wanted to be in the union because it gave me an opportunity to do good work where you really weren't pushed; it wasn't all speed. They realize that you just can't throw it up in a short time and have it look right.

The working conditions, as far as safety, having stewards on the job to watch out for you to make sure everything is safe as it can be—that was my main thing. And benefits. When we worked nonunion, we really didn't have any benefits. We got a raise one time; they gave us a dollar raise. Well, they decided that they were going to take fifty cents and put it in a pension fund and by the time they were done they took the whole dollar. Whereas in the union, at least you can vote on it. It may not go where you want it to, but at least you have the opportunity to vote. In nonunion you didn't. You were on a one-to-one basis. If you wanted anything, you had to go in to ask the boss. Either he says yes or bye. That's the way it is. That was another main reason [to join the union]. I mean you are a union *together;* you're not just an individual fighting for yourself; you're working together striving for the same goals.

Since I've been in the local, I don't think I've ever lost a job because I'm black. The biggest problem is affirmative action. Guys have been in the union for three years and someone [black] comes in and takes a job they think they should have had. It's been a slow process, but some people still have resentment. If we jump the list on them, they feel bad about it. At first I felt bad about it too. But then I think about it on the other side. If I was being treated equal, I might have been in the position to have that job in the first place. It doesn't bother me anymore. I've had the opportunity to go out on jobs as a minority, but I don't want to take those jobs. If they need someone, I want the job, but I don't want to go out strictly as a minority.

When I first came in the local, I had a cold feeling from a lot of the members and the business agents; you could sense it. But over the years it just kind of mellowed out. I mean, they kind of got more used to it; it's not nearly as bad as it once was when I first came in. It's just a feeling that you have. Some of them have gone out of their way to do anything for me. Others have helped me more than they should. When I first started working through the local, I didn't have to join. I could have worked for two years without paying dues. But I didn't want it that way. I said, if I'm going to work in this local, I want to be a part of it. I didn't want to be an outsider looking in.

I'm an easygoing guy; I try to be friends with everybody. The past fifteen years by being in the local I've gained a lot of friends and I believe my union sisters and brothers have accepted me as a hardworking, easygoing guy and not just a minority.

Teri Warren Dominguez

Teri Warren Dominguez is one of sixteen women members of Local 189. She stands five feet ten and a half inches tall and is slim and fairly broad-shouldered for a

Teri Warren Dominguez

woman. Teri, whose father, Dick Warren, is a thirty-five-year veteran union welder, has been working as a pipefitter for eleven years. She is married to another construction worker, Leandro Dominguez, and has two children, Jasmine, aged three, and Daniel, eighteen months. As one of the few women pipefitters, Teri struggles to reconcile her notion of femininity with the challenge of gaining acceptance in a traditionally male occupation. On these and other issues, like so many other Local 189 members, Teri is unafraid to speak her mind.

I've always had male-oriented jobs. I was a security officer, bartender, and then this. I always got along better with men. I was always in the garage with my stepdad. Tools fascinated me; he was always working on something so I was right there with him. Ever since I was a kid, I put all the toys together, and whenever anything had to be fixed, I did it. I always enjoyed it.

I was a store detective when the unions were picketing Kroger's, the supermarket, because they weren't taking union bids. They would go in and fill up carts with stuff and then take it up to the register and leave it. They were doing all kinds of things. I had to go out and take their pictures. So I got to talking to them—because I always talked to everybody—and they told me that the unions were hiring women. We were laughing and stuff and real friendly; I didn't take it seriously. They weren't doing anything, in my opinion, that was wrong. They changed shifts, and the next guy that came on happened to be the head of the apprenticeship school, Dick Patterson. He gave me his card and said to come down in April. This was the first year, 1979, they were going to take women. Everyone knew my dad, and that made it real easy for me.

I did really good on the test, and then they had the interview and I ended up third on the list and I started June 19. I called my dad to tell him about it, and he tried to talk me out of it; he said that's no place for women. He was really against it. I said, "Dad, I'm going to show you that you're wrong. That's all there is to it." For my birthday he got me my first rule and channel locks; that's all the tools you need on the job. The ones everyone else carries are thirteen inches; the ones my dad got me were six inches long. I said "Dad, are you trying to tell me something?"

We're real close now. Ever since I got in the trade, I've gotten to know my dad again. He was my foreman on a couple of jobs. I really like working with him. He's a wonderful fitter. He said, "I'm a thirty-five-year apprentice; I learn something new every day." There are three of us in the family, and I'm really close to my dad and no one else is. I told my dad once, "It's kind of funny but the son you always wanted turned out to be your daughter."

You can't be a priss and be in this job. On the job I'm not always messing with my hair or trying to keep my makeup on. I don't wear makeup to work. If I go to work, I don't carry a brush. I go to work with my hair wet, and after it dries I put it up in a ponytail so it's not driving me crazy. And I wear blue jeans and a T-shirt every day. I had a terrible time my first three years dealing with that. I used to be a cocktail waitress before that. I wore Danskin skirts—they were really sexy and beautiful—and I had nails painted and long. And you go in to charm the men to give you money. And then you go into construction work, and I was working as an apprentice plus serving drinks at night for my first six months. I had a real bad complex because every time I went up on a ladder I would have some guy come up to me, saying, "Hey buddy, where's your foreman?" And it was an honest mistake. I'm built, I'm tall, and I've got blue jeans on and work boots. Finally, I turned around and I told this guy—I was about twenty-four then— "Look buddy, it took me twenty-four years to grow these things, now you better notice them." I've talked to other women in the local, and they went through the same thing about their womanhood. When you're in the trade, you lose it. And it hurt me inside.

I would go into offices, where the women are dressed to kill, and they make maybe five dollars an hour and they buy all their clothes at Lazarus. And finally I came to terms with it because these women would look down at me because I'd have bib overalls on and be filthy dirty crawling underneath floors and stuff. And I say: "I can afford to dress the way you want. I make twice the money you do. I can laugh all the way to the bank." It took me well over three years to come to terms with it. During the day I can't worry about it, but during the night that's when I try to come out. A lot of the women in the local have the same problem.

A lot of women can't take the—it's not harassment from the men—but the jokes and the clowning around and the sexual talk. And me, I'm just the opposite. I love that. I give it right back to them. And that's why I like it. You can be honest and be yourself. All the guys talk about half the time in construction is sex, and if a woman can't handle that, then she's got to get out.

I try to have quick comebacks. Just like they say, I come right back to them. I'm not going to take —— from anybody. I used to be a lot worse when I was younger. I threatened to throw a twenty-four-inch pipe wrench on some guy's head when he was harassing me on the job. It's not sexual harassment, it's just bugging me and being jerks. I think I've been treated probably twenty times better than most women in the local and a lot of it has to do with my attitude because I'm not going to let them mess with me and they know it. I can pack a mean punch. I used to be pretty roughneck when I was younger.

You kind of get crazy and swept up because you're a construction worker and you've got to be like they are. It's not been as bad the last four years because of the laws. People are smarter now; they don't drink as much. Back when I was going through the program, that's all you did. You went to work, you worked your ass off, you went out to lunch, and you usually had three beers and went back.

Thank God, I got away from it; my Tuesdays out are the only nights I really drink. It all changes after you have kids. It was the best thing I did for myself. I became a mother, but I think I became more of a woman; I wasn't into the construction scene as much. I'm [still] into the work. I think I like proving to the guys I can do it, and if I'm in a factory with a lot of guys around, and even women, it tends to make me work harder so I can show them that I can do that stuff and do it good.

About six of us women all were about the same age when we got in—our early twenties. We're all in our early thirties now, and we all have babies. And some are single parents, and the ones that aren't, their husbands aren't real keen on having them going to meetings and drinking with all the guys. You don't get out as easily. I told my husband, "That's *my* night out. I'm going to have some beer and get away from these kids." But I've always gone to meetings. It's important not only for the business at hand but to stay in touch with your brothers. It's hard for women to get out, and I think that they feel very self-conscious going down there. A few even dropped out. They just couldn't take it. I look on it as all fun. It makes me feel good. Hell, after I had kids and I went back to work, I felt like some old woman, fat and worthless, and nobody wants you to work—you should have babies and have stretch marks and all that. They make me feel like a queen on the job. If they didn't mess with me, I wouldn't like the job [smiles].

It's almost like if you work in the trade as a woman, you have to marry someone in the trade because they can't deal with their women coming home dirty—I mean like dirtballs. And I know very few husbands that would put up with their wives getting home at 1:30 or 2:00 in the morning; but my husband has never gotten mad at me, and he deals with it.

I feel like I'm an equal for those eight hours that I'm at work. Actually, I used to tell everybody when I used to wear a hard hat—once you put on a hard hat you don't take your other hat off because you have that hard hat ring—so I used to tell them: "Until I go home and take this hat off, I'm still one of the guys. When I take this hat off, you better treat me like a lady—or else I'll give you one of these" [shows her fist and laughs at herself].

I feel very fortunate to have this job because not very many women are accepted in the local. I have been in for a couple of offices, and for one I lost by one vote. And that really showed me I had a little bit of respect. Next time around I'll probably run again. Just because I lost didn't put me on a downer for the local. I thought I did great. It proved to me that I did have some people standing behind me.

The only regret I have is that I can't come home and slop out and go to sleep. I've got two little ones. I've got to come home and be a mother. I can't just come home and lay around in my easy chair like the guys do and wait for my wife to give me dinner. My husband isn't my wife, he's my husband. So I've got to come home and cook the dinner and feed and bathe the kids. He helps me a lot when he's here, but he's not here all the time. It's a heavy burden. But I really enjoy the job. I don't think I could ever, ever work in an office. I couldn't be confined to a chair. I couldn't work around all women. I like working around men. They make the job real fun. And I like building things, seeing finished products. I like seeing straight, level, and plumb pipe, like five lines running together and looking perfect. I like to know that I fit it.

I think affirmative action is wonderful. Otherwise I wouldn't have my job. I'd probably be making seven dollars an hour at the most or else making tips. But I'll tell you one thing I don't like—the separate list for minorities. I took a minority call once and I was treated like a minority. I have never in my life been treated as a minority. I was treated worse on that job than I've ever been treated.

When a woman takes a new job out of the hall, she has to work twice as hard as any guy. I can't walk onto a job and be accepted right off the bat. After I'll be on the job, they'll say, "Wow, you can really do that job." I'll say, "Well God, I hope so, I've been doing it for eleven years." I feel like an apprentice every time I go on the job. It's the way the men treat you. I love this local and the men in it, but they can't even believe that a woman can read a blueprint. I think all women have that problem.

Fred Scolieri

Fred Scolieri, president of Local 189 (1987–89), was born on the west side of Columbus in the "bottoms" area. His father was a second-generation Italian

Fred Scolieri

immigrant and a plumber, and his mother was from a longtime Ohio family. Before he joined Local 189, he served thirteen months in the Marine Corps in Vietnam, and his experiences have indelibly affected his character and outlook. Fred often presents a gruff, tough, and businesslike exterior to the world. To those who know him, however, he is warmhearted and thoughtful.

I joined the Marine Corps in 1966 with a bunch of my friends after I got out of school. The recruiter told us we were all going to be riflemen and go to Vietnam. We went overseas in November 1966 and got back in December 1967. Probably one of my worst experiences was when we went on a night ambush and it was raining and cold and nasty, and so we started back down the road a little bit early. We were going to head in toward town; it was so dark we couldn't see so we were walking with hands on each other's shoulders. And our patrol crossed with another American patrol. They set up a hasty ambush, and our point man ran into their second man, and their man's rifle hit our man's chest. They killed three or four of us; only two of my patrol didn't get killed or wounded. I hit the ground and saw those tracers coming over my head and I shot in the air and I probably even killed one of our own men. The guy in front of me and the guy behind me got killed. The guy in front of me had a couple of weeks before he would go home. This friend of mine that was in the other patrol, we used to get together when we got back and drink beer. He used to kid me all the time about me shooting him.

My military experience has affected my whole life. I've been somewhere I couldn't get out of and felt like I've been mistreated in a hundred different ways, so I can handle the big things. It's small things that bug me sometimes.

I believe patriotism goes hand in hand with unionism. Unions are American. We fight for things no other groups do. The unions are probably the only ones that ever put a bumper sticker out that says, Buy American cars. They're backers of a lot of good ideas to support the working people. If there is a cause that needs support, you can go to the unions.

I picked up a lot of patriotism in the service, and sometimes it conflicts with ideas that go around. I liked the invasion of Grenada. Others saw it as just bailing out a lot of rich college kids, but I enjoyed that show of force. Oliver North has turned sour, but at the time I sympathized with the things he did. I believe that you can't let communism start in this part of the world, and that's not backed by the Democrats very well. I think of myself only as a Democrat but not so much as to have a turn-the-other-cheek attitude. That's the kind of patriotism I got from the military.

[Regarding racial problems in the union] There's only one color in the Marine Corps, and that's marine green. I know a lot of services were having racial problems, but with the Marine Corps, I like to think that they won't put up with that crap. There's only one color. That's brotherhood. In the union our oath says take care of your brother, find him employment, help him when he needs a hand. Brotherhood, we've got sisters, too, now. A lot more of our people, if they had had more experiences in their life, would understand it rather than not show up at the union meetings and just think that the only reason they're here is for the money; they think that they can get it without us, which is a joke. You can't go out in Columbus and make $20 an hour as a plumber or fitter without this union.

At one time I thought we [in the military] had a relationship that was even stronger than marriage, that's that brotherhood relationship. That's the way it is with the unions. I feel like I can call and get help I need out of them—personal things. I'm just about to drop some information off to a lawyer for a lawsuit from when I fell at Honda three years ago. It's stuff wrote down by a friend of mine in a union building trade here. He went out of his way to help me when I got hurt. And he helped me throughout. Those are the kinds of things you get out of this brotherhood. You can always get a helping hand—if you ask.

There are some negative things about going into the service and going to war. I just got a divorce, and I've read that Vietnam vets have had more problems than others. You tend to be a little more disciplinary. I've been a little more disciplinary with my kids than if I hadn't been in the military. I'm a little more stern.

After coming back from Nam and joining the local, I was fortunate to start my apprenticeship working for a large company, Huffman-Wolfe, the largest firm here in Columbus, which is gone now. I got to go on some of the large jobs, and I got to be around active union men. Being a Marine and playing a little bit of sports at school, I looked up to the guys that were really involved in the union. The word isn't "wild," but the guys that were involved in the union drank a little more, were a little wilder, spoke up, didn't take no crap, and they were good mechanics too. They could do the job as well as anybody, and they weren't scared to say anything. I guess that impressed me. I looked up to these people. They played as hard as they worked. That's probably all the wrong reasons for getting involved, but I was impressed with them; I liked them; they were popular.

Construction is a job a lot of us like. It's not sitting at a desk every day. The more jobs I'm on, the better I like it. It's nice to see something completely different every day; there's challenge every day; you have to think; it's not repetitious; everything around you changes from time to time. It's enjoyable. There's nothing better than working outside on a beautiful day! It's a good business.

The construction trades are very different. There are no paid sick days, no paid vacations. The bad part of it is the weather sometimes and the fact that jobs end. It can be a tough business on the wives. It makes it hard to buy things. You take out a four-year loan and work on a job four days.

[Regarding his position as president] I think that anybody that goes to union meetings and is active thinks about becoming president. To start, I didn't run for anything, but I was picked for the death fund committee. There are lots of committees in our organizations, and some of the smaller ones are pushed onto the kids coming up. There's a lot of people that don't want to become involved, but quite a lot are involved at one time or another. Some get their hands in it, back off, and are supportive. A small group are interested in getting into the politics of the local. The first thing I ran for was vice-president of the local. I think I basically did it because two plumbers were running and I was a pipefitter. Being a young kid, I was running against older members and I didn't make it. When I finally made it to president, it helped that my father had been a member of the local and that I had been active.

Back a long time ago, the president was the top dog, but he's been phased out more and more. [But] I still play a powerful part in the union. As president I'm ex officio member of every committee except the apprenticeship and political action committees. I pick a lot of committees, including the labor-management committee, which I co-chair with the business manager. We have a meeting every three months with the contractors to keep ourselves current, and we handle grievances that come up. And the vice-president of the executive board handles our own members who might go astray. I also chair the union meetings. If anything has to be done, the best place to get it done is on the floor of the meeting. I work out in the field, which means I don't have the time to work on union business during the days.

John Waltz

John Waltz is an intense, outspoken man, deeply impressed with the injustices in American society, in large part because he experienced so many disappointments in

John Waltz

his own life. Born in Belfast, Northern Ireland, in an Irish Catholic family, John grew up in Columbus dreaming of becoming a rock musician. John has many strong opinions about a number of topics, and mostly they come back to unions, the economy, and big business–dominated politics. John has a biting sense of humor in which he is often the butt of the joke as in his comment about his return from San Francisco, where he had hoped to make it in the music business: "I learned the true meaning of success: I went to California in a $3,500 car and came back to Columbus in a $150,000 Greyhound bus."

I was brought into this trade by a friend of mine whose son I grew up with. In high school I took art as a major for three years, went to a special art seminar, played in the band, was a singer. Back in the 1960s in this town, we played for sock hops and teen hops, and we were sponsored by a TV and radio station. Then I went into the army, and when I came out in 1965, Gene Brewer, then business manager of the local and the father of my good friend, asked me what I wanted to do for a living. I was a musician then. He said, "That's OK, but you have to have something you can depend on." So he got me into the trade.

I start my twenty-fifth year in September. I'll be forty-four years old. I never realized that this far down the line the workingman would be so discriminated against, so put against the wall. This country sends a president over to Poland to admire Lech Walesa for protecting the coal miners. If we had a half a million miners on strike, they'd be shot. We have these poor miners in West Virginia protecting their livelihood, their pensions. And all they get is [makes a spitting sound].

We're one of the few unions no one knows anything about. I've never heard anything good said about a union in the *Columbus Dispatch,* particularly a building trades union, in the twenty-five years I've been in the union. Well, here's a union that's existed a hundred years. We get no sick leave, no paid vacations; we go to work—we get paid; we don't go to work—we get nothing. I want people to know that there are labor unions in this country that carry their own people. Discrimination has nothing to do with it. They won't let you get into a situation of dire straits without bending over backward to pull you back out of that to keep your self-esteem and whatever else you call it. These things do exist; it's a genuine brotherhood.

People in this country care only about themselves. It started in California in the 1970s; now it's worked its way into the Midwest. The union cares about everyone. I always wanted to voice an opinion about what I've felt about things. If we don't watch how our unions are treated and the working class is treated in this country, we will die. Sure, we can get cheap labor from whatever country wants to come over here to take menial tasks; sure, we can build robots. But human beings in this country, especially those who replace your toilet and your plumbing in your house, will never be robotized. So why shouldn't they belong to a union that protects them, that gives them a feeling of worth? Sure, you can do away with the Davis-Bacon Act; then what it means is that a guy rolls up into your patio at six o'clock in the morning with a buzz saw and a six-foot ruler in his car and he can recarpenter your house, even though he doesn't know what he's doing. You can have cheap labor and you get exactly what you pay for.

I didn't have much of a father image when I was young. My father wasn't around. Gene Brewer took us on boat outings and ice-skating and to different social functions. He made me part of his family. He helped to raise me, and as I got older he tried to gear me into a situation where I could make a living. I have a strong family relationship to this day with Gene Brewer, he's like an uncle to me. I used to tell him, "I don't know what I would have done if I hadn't got into this." When I die, if the only thing I get is a plaque on that [union hall] wall saying that John Waltz dedicated his life to this organization, then that's a feather in my cap. In this society that doesn't give a damn about anybody else, that's all that exists. These are the basics of the working class in this country.

What's going on in this country is a mockery to the working class. Yuppies can't fix their toilets or put a roof on their houses. They can have a BMW and Jacuzzi or a Steely Dan T-shirt, but they can't repair it. I can repair it. I have no credit cards. It's the consumers who are responsible for the deficit, for the budget and banking deficit. I don't live beyond my means. Most of us—at least 60 percent—in this organization live that way. We live humbly; we live within our means. When we're laid off, our wages are cut in half; unemployment compensation may make the house or car payment, but that's it. The American consumer doesn't realize when he is overdrawn. We've learned to live within our means.

I was a protester in the 1960s even though I was in the army. When I came out of the army, I was involved in protests at the statehouse and in central Ohio. I learned that you can't fight ten billion people in China. My brother and a lot of my friends came back messed up. Fortunately, I was in and out of the army before things really got hot. Some of the men my age realize it was a losing battle, but they didn't realize it at the time. In those days, I had long hair and a beard and played in a rock-and-roll band. I won't say that I was discriminated against, but I wasn't very well understood. Then, long hair was a sign of protest. They said, "What's wrong with this guy?" I was the original hippie, free-lance musician, plumber radical pervert. It's hard to talk of this at age forty-three and having been through it all and having a good reputation now. [It's like] the Bruce Springsteen song about covering up your crap—you covered it up forever, but you can still smell it. I used to be like that. I got a nickname, "Crazy John," because I stood up for my rights in a time of protest and didn't get shoved around.

I had this headstrong belief that I really was going to make it big in the music business. But things didn't work out that way. When I went to Frisco, I thought I could make it. At that point I had been working in the trade twelve years. While I was there, I lost everything I had: my wife, my job, all my possessions. If you heard me sing then, you'd say, "This guy can sing" and I still can.

I'm just learning now how to let things go. It was rough on me. I can show you pictures taken eight years ago, and I didn't have a gray hair on my head. I think it's because of the bitterness and resentment. I've learned that time does heal and that over time people forget. This organization never stopped believing in me; they never threw me out. I come from a family where I don't talk to my brother or sisters. Everybody in my family went to college except me. My one sister teaches school and is married to a college graduate. Another sister manages a chain of small department stores in Boston. My brother graduated from college and he's a computer razzmatazz. And I chose to work with my back and my hands and pursue my music thing. The bitterness and anger stem from that, and I guess I carried it on a little bit too long. If I just had a videotape of what I've seen in the past twenty years, it'd be a hell of a videotape.

From the ground, to the heavens, back to hell, but I've always come back to this. This is always my home, always my family, more of a family to me than my actual flesh and blood. Most people don't look at unions this way. After twenty-four years there is a common denominator. The people here are genuinely my friends. There is a brotherhood here, there is love here. In California you get what they call "Californicated." [Those ideas are] just coming back here now: where no one cared about anyone else. If you're all alone by yourself you're a lump of crap. I don't feel like I'm a lump of crap in here.

David Hinojosa

David is a fourth-year apprentice born in Columbus and of Hispanic descent. At the age of thirty-one, David is an independent thinker who identifies strongly with the union. But like many of the local's present officials, who were elected as reformers, David insists that the union live up to its own ideals.

I used to work on cars—I'd do anything mechanical—and was up to ten bucks an hour, about twenty-five thousand bucks a year. I wanted more money, plus I wanted a trade. I started trying to get in in 1980. I was twenty-one then, but unemployment was really bad. I was 486 on the apprenticeship list. My dad wasn't in the union to get me in. When I applied, I put "white," even though my mom is from Puerto Rican ancestry and my dad is Chilean. He joined the air force and

David Hinojosa

they moved to Columbus to be near Rickenbacker Air Force Base. They [the Joint Apprenticeship Committee] never took apprentices that year. I was way high on the list. There was five hundred people laid off. I tried the next time around and didn't do any better. It took me until '86 to get in. And *then* I put down that I was Hispanic.

I was getting old then. I'd say that's the reason I got in. I was qualified to do the work. I was older. Most of the guys in the apprenticeship school are really young. They're just there to work; they're not serious yet, like in school, they're just trying to get by. Some of them are serious, but a lot of them aren't. I had worked on cars for almost ten years and I had mechanical aptitude. I did real well on the test. You had to take the test before you could see the apprenticeship board. I took in all those letters they had been sending me and said, "Listen, if you don't want me to get in, just tell me now and I won't come back." Later, Patterson called me at work and left a message to come in. I thought about it for a day because it would mean a cut in pay from $10 to $5.75 an hour. I thought, I can sit here and make good money or I can learn the trade and earn more in the end and learn something also. I thought, even if it doesn't work out in the end, I can learn this stuff and always go back and work on cars. It was just building my knowledge.

I'm not much for school. I could have done better in high school, but back then all we did was party, go out and cut school. I wasn't a serious school person. That's just the way we did it. When I got in the trade, I really enjoyed it because I was grown up by then and I tried to learn.

They called me up and I went to this PPG (Pittsburgh Plate Glass) job in Delaware [Ohio]. It was strange. I pulled up in the parking lot and half knew where to go. All I knew was I was to work for Limbach Company. I seen guys walking in; it was all new. I was working for Mike Kerber; he was a welder. There were about a hundred guys in the fab shop. It was a big job; I'd never seen anything like that. It was pretty interesting. I didn't get to do a whole lot. I was always with a journeyman. We did stainless steel work. I had to fit for a welder. I had to cut the pipe and make sure it was squared up. We took measurements and put up hangers. We were putting in pumping stations for semis to back up into. Hooking up all these valves, pretty much fabbing it all up. They had a general idea what they wanted; they had a picture, but you still had to make a lot of adjustments; that's what pipefitting is all about. There might be something in the way; there's other crafts in there working too and sometimes you have to work around each other. We had to climb up in the air on the steel. That was kind of scary, but it was kind of neat. I enjoyed it because it was like being a kid again, doing wild stuff. Me and my friends was always into things like that. Plus I was learning too. Learning how to weld a little bit. Just by practicing when they was on break. I'd pick up the torch and weld.

Then I started going to school. It was April when I got in so there was only four or five classes left. There were two other guys there, and we didn't do a whole lot till the next year. In basic class we learned the different fittings and how to run a pipe machine, how to cut a thread, how to take pipe measurements. There are different ways you can use a tape, a lot of handy, quick math, learning the quick and accurate way. Patterson let us weld a couple of times and [taught us] how to strike an arc. We learned how we could be useful on the job basically. Got familiar with the tools and how you do things and then you pick up most of it on the job. They showed us a little bit about blueprints and how to read them. Once you started handling the stuff, you understood it. I think they could do a little better. Next year they're going to get people to go two nights a week. It was thirty some weeks [of training], a long time.

I got along with everybody pretty good. You're an apprentice and you do pretty much what they tell you to do. You don't have much to say in whether it could be done some other way. In my instance I didn't know some other way. You did a lot of crap jobs, like sweeping up or picking up, or cleaning, stuff that *they* won't do [laughs]. But there's a lot of journeymen that'll do anything. Like cut holes in the wall. Working with a welder, I learned to fit. People were pretty helpful. A lot of guys wouldn't show you anything. You'd have to watch what they're doing and then learn it on your own. They see it as protecting their job, keeping you as dumb as they can so you won't be able to take their job. A lot of guys, they'll show you everything there is to know about it, they don't care. But they don't have time often because they don't always foresee what you should be doing.

But now in my fourth year, I know quite a bit—I don't think I'll know it all, not ever—but I've got a real good grasp of most things. After a while you automatically know things, like in a steam system: there's a condensate and a trap and you got to have a union and shutoff valves and bypasses. Knowing what wrenches to get. You have to think in advance so you don't have to make so many trips. They can't teach all that stuff in school.

Second year was welding. Only one night a week, you couldn't learn that much. I liked that class; we learned a lot about safety; you need that on the job; it's dangerous every day. We did a little book work, learned the principles of it: cutting, and braising, and welding. We went into our little booths and started welding away and kept messing up, and eventually you got better. We got tested to see how well we were doing. I don't do any welding on the job; they don't let me; maybe once in a while. They should let you learn more. I'd like to do more welding. I got the steps in school, but I learned from my mistakes on the job. It's completely different welding on the job. [In school] you learn what size rod and what heat to use, how far away from the pipe to get, how you're supposed to angle your rod. It sounded pretty good, but it was hard to do [in practice].

My second year I worked for Limbach. They laid me and Pam [another apprentice] off and we started at ATF cause they needed minorities. It was the middle of the winter, freezing, mud up to your knees; when you put them big boots on, it would suck them off if you stepped in a mud puddle. I was a complete "gofer" there, didn't learn anything except how to drive a truck in the mud, which is beneficial. I knocked a lot of holes in the wall and froze my ass off. I watched them sweat copper and clean fittings.

Plumbing work is smaller than what we worked on at Limbach, mostly four inches and below. I did learn how to hook up heaters, how to hook up all the little individual units. It's a lot different than working for a big piping outfit like Limbach that does process piping. I learned quite a bit about plumbing, so much more than those other [apprentices] that just did pipefitting. They hated plumbing, cause they didn't know what the stuff was. I had a hell of a good idea. I did bathrooms. I worked at the Limited, that place was huge; we put in great big roof drains, roughed in bathrooms, drinking fountains, urinals, and such. They start trusting you more. Most of the time the journeymen hold you back. You really have to know what you're doing cause you can break those toilets and sinks pretty easily. I think they should make you work for different companies. They do somewhat, but it's nice to get a well-rounded experience. I can understand why those guys didn't like plumbing.

My third year I was working down on campus on the Wexner Center. I was pretty knowledgeable by then, but I couldn't do a whole lot. They had me handling material. I would have to find ways to get it downstairs. I learned about the different kinds of fittings. The beginning of this year I really felt like I knew what was going on, like I could help anybody do anything, not be stupid. Now I've done so much, I start thinking in advance.

It's a hard trade. It sounds easy. People laugh, they don't know what it is. As far as the knowledge goes, it's great, for a person like myself—I didn't do real well at school and I didn't want to go to college. I wish I would have, but I like working with my hands. I just know so much more now. I could fix something at home. Plus, I could make money at it. If the union was gone tomorrow, you'd still have all your knowledge. It's like a degree at school, something you can fall back on. There's so much there: plumbing, welding, heating, air conditioning, and pneumatics. Anybody that can learn all that, they're doing real well. That's why I like it. Every year I'm doing something different. If you're a good worker, you can pretty much stay working most of the time. There's a lot of guys that get laid off, but most of the companies keep you around if you're a good worker.

I hate that minority thing. You should be able to do the work, and that's the bottom line. A lot of guys, that's a rough spot. At the last [union] meeting they initiated four apprentices, two girls and a black guy and white guy, and one of the Limbach crew that was surrounding me, said, "Now the white guy's a minority." I won a T-shirt in the drawing saying, "Made in America, American Pride," and I'm a minority and the guys were giving me crap. It's good-natured, but I get tired of hearing it. They call me "Taco," that's my nickname now. I've had a lot of harassment, but I've never let it get to me. All I worry about is doing the work. That minority thing is a big problem in our local. Some minorities don't do anything [at work]; [they feel that] they don't have to worry because they are a minority. That's no way to be at all. Pam is a dynamic worker, but you should have heard the stuff she had to put up with. But if you're an apprentice, you have to put up with it.

What do I think about unions? I'd hear of unions but didn't really think about them. A lot of people would tell me how bad it was. "Aw, you don't want to get in no union, they just take your money." We have to pay dues, and it's expensive, but I like it. I think it's a good program. I just think it's terrible that only about a third [of members] go to union meetings at most, and that was a contract meeting. It's a good union and I'm proud of it, but I don't think it's very strong. If it came down to working or not working, a lot of people would probably be working somewhere else. If they're serious about it, they'd come to meetings. I hate to say—it makes me feel bad—but that's true, and I always get on them journeymen at work, at Limbach. Most of them guys have been there forever; they're "steady Eddies," and they don't go to the meetings. They don't care, cause they know they're going to be working tomorrow. But I still believe that you should be union, not company-oriented.

These guys forget they're in the union. I've seen guys do ironwork [outside their jurisdiction] putting in beams and stuff and not even think twice about it, and the steward is working alongside them. That ain't no way to be. And here they bitch about people doing piping work and yet they'll do anything they can do. That ain't the way it's supposed to be. That's what we've been taught in apprenticeship. Some guys use their trucks to haul things around. It's just not serious. I'm sure there's a lot of guys that might die for the union, but not the majority.

Like when we had that [handbilling] at Sears. That was a pretty serious thing. But we didn't have that many guys there. We could have had the whole hall down there. They'd have really been noticing us. The whole twelve hundred of us, can you imagine us in Sears! But there wasn't. In Chicago they're serious all the way, those guys stick together. They take care of business. We've gotten away from that here. I think we're getting weaker and weaker. I hope it doesn't continue.

Appendix

Meeting Halls of Local Union 189, Columbus, Ohio

1903–4: 31½ W. Broad Street

1904–7: 17½ E. Town Street

1907–12: 40 E. Chestnut Street

1912–13: 17½ E. Chestnut Street

1913–14: 17½ E. Town Street

1914–23: Fink Hall, 21 N. Front Street

1923–25: Federation of Labor Hall, 50½ W. Gay Street

1925–27: Eagles Hall, 771 N. High Street

1927–30: 261½ High Street

1930–36: Carpenter Hall, 8 E. Chestnut Street

1936–50: Carpenter Hall, 293 E. Rich Street

1951–52: 250 Donaldson Street

1952–64: 555 E. Rich Street

1964–81: Richard Anderson Hall, 841 Alton Avenue

1981–present: 1250 Kinnear Road

Local 189 Officers

Presidents

Martin Stai, 1899

Frank P. Tully, 1900–1901

Mike Ginley, 1902

Len Harris, 1903

George Conklin, 1903

Harvey Dunn, 1903

Mike Ginley, 1904

Tom Martin, 1905

Albert Lowe, 1905

Jim Hardy, 1906

Mears, 1906

Mike Ginley, 1907, 1910

Thomas Birch, 1907

Wheppley, 1908

J. Rhoenbeck, 1908

N. Perry, 1909

Albert M. McBride, 1909–11

unknown, 1912–16

Kaiser, 1917

Adrian Smith, 1918

Shaw, 1919

Albert M. McBride, 1919

Lee A. Brown, 1920

Harry T. Jones, 1921

J. Dunnigan, 1922

F. R. Smith, 1923

Charles A. Seddon, 1924

Thomas Aitkin, 1925, 1926

Albert M. McBride, 1927

Arthur M. Barr, 1928–29

Francis Graham, 1929–30

Early, 1931

Francis Graham, 1931–32

Nolan Perry, 1933–35

Art Doersham, 1936–37

Forest Lewis, 1938

Wilburt Jenkins, 1939

William Beckel, 1940–42

Art Doersham, 1942

R. S. Kearney, 1943–44

William Beckel, 1945–53

James Colburn, 1954–55

William Beckel, 1956–59

Richard Anderson, 1960–64

James Heinmiller, 1964–65

Eugene Evans, 1966–67

Danie Lewis, 1968–70

Jim Ely, 1971

John Noll, 1972–76

John "Gus" Naegele, 1977–79

James Brennan, 1980–82

Dick Patterson, 1983–84

Bob Meredith, 1984–85

Fred Scolieri, 1986–88

Pat Ferry, 1988–91

Mike Kelley, 1992–

Business Agents

Charles A. McAndrews, 1901

Al Seddon, 1901–8

Thomas Birch, 1908–29

Arthur M. Barr, 1929–31

Albert McBride, 1931–35

Floyd Geiger, 1935–39

Francis E. Graham, 1940–43

Ed James, 1943–53

Richard J. Liddil, 1954–63

Ed Scanlon (assistant), 1955–56

Frank Crowley (assistant), 1956–69

Joseph J. Snyder, 1968–70

Danie Lewis, 1971–85

Bill McAfee, 1971–75

Bob Dyer, 1977–82

Dudley Steiner, 1977–82

Guy Holmes, 1982–85

Bill Steinhauser, 1983–89

Jim Young, 1986–91

Bob Meredith, 1986–89

Fred Scolieri, 1992–

Business Managers

Dudley Steiner, 1964–75

Gene Brewer, 1975–77

Gene Minix, 1977–

Financial Secretaries

Edward Mills, 1899

J. Fortner, 1900

J. Hardy, 1903

William Schneider, 1904

Roy Snyder, 1904–5

R. Jones, 1905

A. H. Nippert, 1905

Edward Rupprecht, 1905–8

W. K. Noble, 1908–14

Frank O. Hendershott, 1914–15

Philip S. Dreher, 1915–20

William G. Stai, 1920–29

Business agent did job, 1929–31

Joe Schneider, 1931–41

Ray Middendorf, 1941–47

Financial Secretary-Treasurers

Ray Middendorf, 1948–51

Joseph J. Sins, 1951–57

John Heinmiller, 1957–71

Charles Gronbach, 1972

Union Jurisdiction
LU 189, Columbus, Ohio

Charter Date:
December 9, 1899
May 4, 1965: Metal Trades added to charter

Mergers:
September 5, 1929: LU 216, Columbus, Ohio
August 1, 1963: LU 574, Marion, Ohio
June 1, 1969: LU 723, Chillicothe, Ohio
(extended LU 189 jurisdiction to include Ross County)
January 1, 1974: LU 271, Newark, Ohio
July 1, 1987: LU 97, Springfield, Ohio (Territory and members divided between LUs
162, 776, 189, and 577. LU 189 received that portion in Madison County.)

General Jurisdiction:
1937: LU 189 received jurisdiction over Marion, Ohio
1938: LU 189 received jurisdiction over Lancaster, Ohio
1941: LU 189 received jurisdiction over Circleville, Ohio
1956: LU 189 received jurisdiction over Logan, Ohio
1967: Marion County declared open territory
1971: LU 189 received jurisdiction over Marion County

Convention Delegates, 1900–1986

Date	Delegates
1900, August 6–11	No delegate
1901, August 19–24	No delegate
1902, August 18–23	No delegate
1904, August 15–20	No delegate
1906, September 17–28	Michael Ginley
1908, September 21–29	Michael Ginley
1910, September 19–27	Michael Ginley
1913, August 18–25	P. Dreher
1917, August 13–21	Michael Ginley
1921, September 19–24	H. T. Jones
1924, September 15–20	H. T. Jones and Hugo Kaiser

Date	Delegates
1928, September 17–21	Thomas P. Birch and C. A. Seddon
1938, September 12–16	Thomas P. Birch
1942, September 14–17	Thomas P. Birch, D. E. James, William J. Bechel
1946, September 9–13	No delegates
1951, September 10–14	D. E. James, Roy Mount, A. Wohlfarth, W. J. Beckel, E. J. Early
1956, August 13–17	Richard J. Liddil, Martin C. Scanlan, Daniel C. Work, John E. Heinmiller, Jr., and William J. Beckel, Sr.
1961, August 7–11	Daniel C. Work, Frank J. Crowley, Dudley Steiner, Richard J. Liddil, Lawrence Sweeney, Richard C. Anderson, Eugene F. Brewer, and Michael J. Ginley, Jr.
1966, August 8–12	F. J. Crowley, E. W. Evans, J. E. Heinmiller, Jr., D. Lewis, J. J. Snyder, D. H. Steiner, L. Sweeney, Sr., L. J. Sweeney, Jr., and D. C. Work
1971, August 2–5	James Brennan, Eugene F. Brewer, Robert H. Dyer, James E. Ely, Thomas J. Killilea, Danie G. Lewis, Gail W. McAfee, Denis Reynolds, Joseph H. Snyder, Dudley H. Steiner, and Lawrence J. Sweeney, Jr.
1976, August 16–20	Eugene F. Brewer, Robert H. Dyer, James E. Ely, Charles Gronbach, Thomas J. Killilea, Danie G. Lewis, Gail W. McAfee, John C. Naegele, John F. Noll, Dudley H. Steiner, Lawrence J. Sweeney, Jr., Lawrence J. Sweeney, Sr., and Arnold Zack
1981, August 10–14	William D. Beal, James R. Brennan, Robert H. Dyer, Ronald E. Graves, Charles Gronbach, Guy R. Holmes, Danie G. Lewis, Max W. McCalla, Eugene Minix, John C. Naegele, Richard L. Patterson, Dudley H. Steiner, Lawrence J. Sweeney, Jr., Arnold Zack
1986, July 28–August 1	William D. Beal, Eugene F. Brewer, Patrick T. Ferry, Darrell A. Gammell, Charles Gronbach, Robert J. Merideth, Eugene Minix, Fredrick C. Scolieri, Henry W. Steinhausser, Lawrence J. Sweeney, Jr., Louis P. Volpe, James H. Young, Arnold Zack

Membership, 1900–1989

Year	As of Month	Membership
1900	June	37
1901	June	79

Year	As of Month	Membership
1902	June	85
1904	June	86
1906		LU 189 sent 1 delegate to the convention. Per the UA constitution each local with a minimum of 25 members was entitled to 1 delegate. Locals having a minimum of 200 members were entitled to 2 delegates and 1 additional delegate for every 100 members above 200.
1908		Ditto 1906
1910		Ditto 1906
1913		Ditto 1906
1917		Ditto 1906
1921	September	LU 189 sent 1 delegate to the convention. Per the UA constitution each local with a minimum of 20 members was entitled to 1 delegate and 1 additional delegate for every 100 members above the initial 20.
1924	September	LU 189 sent 2 delegates to the convention. Basis of representation the same as 1921.
1928	September	Ditto 1924.
1929	June	196 + 28 = 224*
1930	September	180 + 31 = 211*
1931	June	160 + 19 = 179*
1932	June	145 + 15 = 160*
1933	June	124 + 15 = 139*
1934	June	121 + 9 = 130*
1935	June	119 + 3 = 122*
1936	June	107 + 12 = 119*
1937	June	132 + 1 = 133*
1938	June	150 + 2 = 152*
1939	June	183 + 1 = 184*
1940	June	193 + 15 = 208*
1941	June	228 + 4 = 232*
1942	June	309 + 1 = 310*
1943	June	334 + 1 = 335*
1946	June	LU 189 sent no delegate to the convention. It is possible that a delegate from another local also represented 189. Basis of representation the same as 1921.
1951	June	LU 189 sent 5 delegates to the convention. Basis of representation the same as 1921.
1956		LU 189 sent 5 delegates to the convention. Basis of representation the same as 1921.

Year	As of Month	Membership		
1960	September	765		
1961	December	726 BTJ + 41 BTA	=	767
1962	June	717 BTJ + 49 BTA	=	766
1962	December	726 BTJ + 44 BTA	=	770
1963	June	719 BTJ + 40 BTA	=	759
1963	December	739 BTJ + 39 BTA	=	778
1964	June	730 BTJ + 42 BTA	=	772
1964	December	735 BTJ + 44 BTA	=	779
1965	June	765 BTJ + 46 BTA	=	811
1965	December	787 BTJ + 50 BTA	=	837
1966	May	788 BTJ + 57 BTA + 18 MTJ	=	863
1966	June	793 BTJ + 56 BTA + 18 MTJ	=	867
1966	December	819 BTJ + 47 BTA + 53 MTJ	=	819
1967	June	829 BTJ + 54 BTA + 57 MTJ	=	940
1969	June	868 BTJ + 74 BTA + 89 MTJ	=	1,031
1969	December	974 BTJ + 67 BTA + 92 MTJ	=	1,133
1970	June	968 BTJ + 68 BTA + 90 MTJ	=	1,126
1970	December	953 BTJ + 68 BTA + 101 MTJ	=	1,122
1971	June	941 BTJ + 71 BTA + 93 MTJ	=	1,105
1971	December	939 BTJ + 81 BTA + 76 MTJ	=	1,076
1972	June	925 BTJ + 67 BTA + 58 MTJ	=	1,050
1972	December	929 BTJ + 76 BTA + 65 MTJ	=	1,070
1973	June	951 BTJ + 56 BTA + 80 MTJ	=	1,087
1973	December	1,046 BTJ + 54 BTA + 105 MTJ	=	1,205
1974	June	1,047 BTJ + 49 BTA + 110 MTJ	=	1,206
		Local 271 merged with Local 189 Jan 1, 1974—Membership—95		
1974	December	1,050 BTJ + 43 BTA + 121 MTJ	=	1,214
1975	June	1,045 BTJ + 50 BTA + 112 MTJ	=	1,207
1975	December	1,045 BTJ + 53 BTA + 138 MTJ	=	1,236
1976	June	1,039 BTJ + 52 BTA + 143 MTJ	=	1,234
1976	December	1,067 BTJ + 27 BTA + 137 MTJ	=	1,231
1977	June	1,058 BTJ + 42 BTA + 124 MTJ	=	1,224
1977	December	1,051 BTJ + 41 BTA + 156 MTJ	=	1,248
1978	June	1,059 BTJ + 56 BTA + 146 MTJ	=	1,261
1978	December	1,063 BTJ + 45 BTA + 148 MTJ	=	1,256
1979	June	1,064 BTJ + 50 BTA + 179 MTJ + 4 MTA	=	1,297
1979	December	1,070 BTJ + 65 BTA + 174 MTJ + 3 MTA	=	1,312
1980	June	1,069 BTJ + 76 BTA + 166 MTJ + 2 MTA	=	1,313
1980	December	1,066 BTJ + 79 BTA + 193 MTJ + 2 MTA	=	1,340
1981	June	1,077 BTJ + 75 BTA + 198 MTJ + 2 MTA	=	1,352

Year	As of Month	Membership	
1981	December	1,131 BTJ + 71 BTA + 208 MTJ + 2 MTA	= 1,412
1982	June	1,139 BTJ + 74 BTA + 155 MTJ + 1 MTA	= 1,369
1982	December	1,133 BTJ + 65 BTA + 141 MTJ + 2 MTA	= 1,341
1983	June	1,159 BTJ + 40 BTA + 139 MTJ	= 1,338
1983	December	1,155 BTJ + 31 BTA + 149 MTJ	= 1,335
1984	June	1,143 BTJ + 39 BTA + 151 MTJ	= 1,333
1984	December	1,131 BTJ + 43 BTA + 144 MTJ + 1 MTA	= 1,319
1985	June	1,130 BTJ + 34 BTA + 116 MTJ + 1 MTA	= 1,281
1985	December	1,121 BTJ + 38 BTA + 110 MTJ + 1 MTA	= 1,270
1986	June	1,114 BTJ + 74 BTA + 101 MTJ + 1 MTA	= 1,290
1986	December	1,107 BTJ + 78 BTA + 100 MTJ + 1 MTA	= 1,286
1987	June	1,123 BTJ + 86 BTA + 99 MTJ	= 1,308
1987	December	1,120 BTJ + 80 BTA + 102 MTJ	= 1,302
1988	June	1,121 BTJ + 81 BTA + 101 MTJ	= 1,303

*(Membership within three months) + (Membership within one year) = TOTAL; BTJ = Building Trades Journeyman; BTA = Building Trades Apprentice; MTJ = Metal Trades Journeyman; MTA = Metal Trades Apprentice

Bibliography

Introduction: For my conception of craft I have relied on Michael J. Piore and Charles F. Sabel, *Second Industrial Divide: Possibilities for Prosperity* (New York: Basic Books, 1984); and Robert Max Jackson, *The Formation of Craft Labor Markets* (Orlando, Fla.: Academic Press, 1984). On construction work in particular I have relied on Herbert A. Applebaum, *Royal Blue: The Culture of Construction Workers* (New York: Holt, Rinehart and Winston, 1981); William Haber, *Industrial Relations in the Building Industry* (Cambridge, Mass.: Harvard University Press, 1930); and Mark Erlich, *With Our Hands: The Story of the Carpenters in Massachusetts* (Philadelphia: Temple University Press, 1986). David Montgomery summarizes the history of construction workers and their unions in the 1865–1920 period in *The Fall of the House of Labor: The Workplace, the State, and American Labor Activism, 1865–1925* (Cambridge: Cambridge University Press, 1987). An excellent case study of a local union of plumbers can be found in *The Worker Views His Union* (Chicago: University of Chicago Press, 1958) by Joel Seidman, Jack London, Bernard Karsh, and Daisy L. Tagliacozzo. Quotations on apprenticeship are from *Your Heritage and Future in the Pipe Trades* (Washington, D.C.: National Joint Steamfitter-Pipefitter Apprenticeship Committee, 1985).

Chapter 1, Windows into the Union: The accounts in this chapter were based on the author's observations and conversations with members of Local 189 of the UA. Statistics on construction workers' safety are from "An Interview with Bob Georgine," *UA Journal*, April 1990.

Chapter 2, The Power of Organization, 1889–1902: Craft and union developments are discussed authoritatively in Martin Segal, *Rise of the United Association: National Unionism in the Pipe Trades, 1884–1924* (Cambridge, Mass.: Wertheim Committee, Harvard University, 1970), chapters 1 and 2; John H. Ashworth, *The Helper and American Trade Unions,* Johns Hopkins University Studies in Historical and Political Science, Series 33, No. 3 (Baltimore: Johns Hopkins University Press, 1915), chapters 1–4. UA President John S. Kelly's testimony, which includes discussion of the exclusive agreement, is found in the *Report of the Industrial Commission of Capital and Labor Employed in Manufactures and General Business* Vol. 7 (Washington, D.C.: U.S. Government Printing Office, 1901); quote from *Official Handbook of the United Association of Journeymen Plumbers, Gas Fitters, Steam Fitters and Steam Fitters' Helpers of the United States and Canada* (UA, 1893). The description of lead wiping is based on an interview with Dick Patterson, apprenticeship training coordinator and member, Local 189.

On developments in Columbus see Betty Garrett and Edward R. Lentz, *Columbus: America's Crossroads* (Tulsa, Okla.: Continental Heritage Press, 1980), chapters 5 and 6. Some material on the background of unions in Columbus is from "Columbus Timesheet: A Chronological History of Labor in Ohio's Capital, 1812–1992," by Warren R. Van Tine (manuscript in possession of author). See also published census material in *Eleventh Census of the United States, 1890:* Vol. 3, *Statistics of Population,* pp. 569, 656, 657.

The Gompers letter is found in *The Samuel Gompers Papers,* Vol. 2: *The Early Years of the American Federation of Labor, 1887–1890,* ed. Stuart B. Kaufman (Urbana: University of Illinois Press, 1987), pp. 365, 366. On the union in the early 1890s I have relied on reports and letters in the *UA Journal,* in particular November and December 1892. Day-to-day events can be followed in the *Columbus Dispatch* and the *Daily Ohio State Journal.* The 1894 Trade and Labor Assembly constitution is found in *History of the Trades Unions of Columbus* (Columbus: Franklin Printing Company, 1895). Biographical information on Louis Bauman is from *Franklin County at the Beginning of the Twentieth Century* (Columbus: Historical Publishing Company, 1901), p. 424. A general account of events in the American labor movement can be found in Foster Rhea Dulles and Melvyn Dubofsky, *Labor in America: A History,* 4th ed. (Arlington Heights, Ill.: Harlan Davidson, 1984).

The history of Locals 189 and 216 after 1899 is based primarily on minutes of the meetings of Local 189 (in possession of Local 189) and the *UA Journal,* particularly July 1901 and June 1902; also the *Columbus Dispatch.* Mike Ginley is remembered by his son, Mike Ginley, Jr., in an interview.

Chapter 3, The Union Takes Shape, 1901–1945: For a general survey of structural developments in unions in this era see Warren R. Van Tine, *The Making of a Labor Bureaucrat: Union Leadership in the United States, 1870–1920* (Amherst: University of Massachusetts Press, 1973). Developments within Local 189 and Local 216 are followed in Local 189's minutes and in the *UA Journal;* quotes are found in issues for March and September 1903, April 1905, and October 1915. National developments and jurisdictional disputes are discussed in Segal, *Rise of the United Association.* The 1904 strike can be followed in the *Columbus Dispatch,* particularly April 16, 24, and 28, May 11, and July 19, 1904. The streetcar strike is discussed in Sidney L. Harring, *Policing a Class Society: The Experience of American Cities, 1865–1915* (New Brunswick, N.J.: Rutgers University Press, 1983), pp. 137–39, and Van Tine, "Columbus Timesheet." Quotes from representatives to the state Building Trades Council are found in *Proceedings of the Fourth Annual Convention of the Ohio State Building Trades Council Held at Central Labor Union Hall, Toledo, Ohio Oct. 5th, 6th, 1916* (Columbus: Ohio Building and Construction Trades Council, 1917). Also see the proceedings of the seventh convention held at Zanesville, Ohio, in 1919.

Background material on World War I through the Great Depression in Columbus is found in Garrett and Lentz, *Columbus,* chapters 7 and 8; in Henry L. Hunker, *Industrial Evolution of Columbus, Ohio* (Columbus: Ohio State University Bureau of Business Research, 1958); and in Van Tine, "Columbus Timesheet." The story about Louis Bauman is from an interview with Jane Heinmiller. Details on the 1930s are from interviews with Francis Wolfe and Matt Roberts. Collective bargaining developments are covered in Local 189 minutes and reports of the general organizer in the *UA Journal.* On apprenticeship see the *UA Journal,* July 1926, October 1927, June 1928, March 1939; and William Haber and Harold M. Levinson, *Industrial Relations and Productivity in the Building Trades* (Ann Arbor: Bureau of Industrial Relations, 1956), chapter 6. Developments in the American labor movement in the 1930s are summarized in Dulles and Dubofsky, *Labor in America.* On relations between the Columbus BTC and Local 189 see Schlenzig to Durkin, March 24, 1941; Durkin to Schlenzig, March 26, 1942, and miscellaneous documents included in letters, Local 189 letters, Reel 6, *Local Union Letters* (microfilm, UA Archives, Washington, D.C.). On wages during the Depression see "Decision of the Wage Adjustment Board, Case No. 1157 Pertaining to Federal Construction Projects in the Matter of Request for Wage Adjustment by United Association of Journeymen Plumbers and Steam Fitter, Local 189," Wage Adjustment Board, U.S. Department of Labor, September 23, 1943. The history of the U.A. since 1924 is covered by Barbara Griffith, *The United Association, 1924–1989: A Study in the History of North American Craft Unionism* (Washington, D.C.: Kelly Press, 1991).

Chapter 4, Building a Stronger and Fairer Union, 1945–1973: This chapter is based on the *UA Journal,* Local 189 minutes, Local 189 contracts, court decrees, other documents in the union's archives and statistics supplied by UA headquarters. It also relies heavily on interviews and discussions with Charlie Gronbach, Gene Minix, Francis Wolfe, Dick Patterson, and Mary Ann Coyle (UA archivist). Also important were interviews with Greg Murphy and Ernie Ware. On developments in Columbus see Garrett and Lentz, *Columbus,* chapter 9. Employment and income data for the year 1950 are from United States Census,

1950, *Detailed Characteristics of Population, Ohio,* Report P-C35 (Washington, D.C.: U.S. Government Printing Office, 1953), p. 399.

Chapter 5, A Fight for Survival: The Nonunion Challenge, 1970–1989: Bottom-up organizing is discussed in "Bottom-Up Organizing in the Trades: An Interview with Mike Lucas, IBEW Director of Organizing," in *Labor Research Review,* no. 12 (Fall 1988), pp. 21–36. The 1970 residential agreement is discussed in "MCACO: The Industry's First Residential Agreement," *PHC-Business,* September 1972, pp. 23–29. Open-shop trends in Columbus and in the nation are summarized in Herbert R. Northrup, *Open Shop Construction Revisited* (Philadelphia: Wharton Publishing Co., 1984); and in Clinton C. Burdon and Raymond E. Leavitt, *Union and Open Shop Construction* (Lexington, Mass.: D. C. Heath, Lexington Books, 1980). Also see "Reflections of a President," *Mechanical Contractor,* May 1970, pp. 28–31. Local agreements can be followed in the Bureau of National Affairs, *Construction Labor Review,* as well as in Local 189 contracts and minutes. Union developments during the administration of Gene Minix can be followed best in the union's newsletter, the *Open Line,* in the union's archives. The French Market affair can be followed in the *Columbus Citizens-Journal* September 15, 1972; October 24, 1972; October 25, 1972; October 27, 1972; and the *Columbus Evening Dispatch,* October 24, 1972, and October 25, 1972. Prospects for building trades union "market recovery" are discussed in "Toning up Union Muscles," *Engineering News Record,* April 26, 1990. This chapter also relied on interviews with Bob Dyer, Charlie Gronbach, Gene Minix, Sam Shuman, James Croson, and Dick Patterson.

Index

About the Author

Richard Schneirov received his Ph.D. from Northern Illinois University and was awarded a Fulbright grant the following year. He is now an associate professor of United States History at Indiana State University. He has previously written a history of the carpenters' union in Chicago.